Rev. John Potter

Reminiscences of the Civil War in the United States

Including also an account of a visit to the battlegrounds of Tennessee and Georgia in 1895

and a memorial sermon, preached at Montezuma, Iowa

Rev. John Potter

Reminiscences of the Civil War in the United States
Including also an account of a visit to the battlegrounds of Tennessee and Georgia in 1895 and a memorial sermon, preached at Montezuma, Iowa

ISBN/EAN: 9783743368712

Manufactured in Europe, USA, Canada, Australia, Japa

Cover: Foto ©ninafisch / pixelio.de

Manufactured and distributed by brebook publishing software (www.brebook.com)

Rev. John Potter

Reminiscences of the Civil War in the United States

REMINISCENCES

OF THE

CIVIL WAR IN THE UNITED STATES,

BY

REV. JOHN POTTER.

OF THE

METHODIST EPISCOPAL CHURCH,

INCLUDING ALSO AN ACCOUNT OF A
VISIT TO THE BATTLE GROUNDS
OF TENNESSEE AND
GEORGIA IN 1895.

AND

A MEMORIAL SERMON,

PREACHED AT

MONTEZUMA, IOWA.

MAY 26TH, 1895.

OSKALOOSA, IOWA:
THE GLOBE PRESSES,
1897.

TO MY WIFE,

ANGELINA,

WHO FOR MORE THAN THIRTY YEARS
HAS SHARED WITH ME THE BUR-
DENS AND BLESSINGS OF LIFE,
AS A TRUE HELPMEET,

THESE PAGES

ARE AFFECTIONATELY INSCRIBED.

TABLE OF CONTENTS.

CHAPTER I.

The political campaign of 1860. Shaking hands with Abraham Lincoln. Impressions on the probabilities of war. Enlistment. Drilling and organization of the One Hundred and First Illinois Volunteers. Pages 13-19.

CHAPTER II.

In camp at Jacksonville, Ills. Order to leave for the seat of war. Parting scene. Arrival at Cairo. Guarding prisoners. The jokes of the soldiers. Pages 20-27.

CHAPTER III.

Leave Cairo. Columbus, detained there. Experience with "graybacks." An alarm in camp. Cruel treatment of negroes. Arrive at Holly Springs, Mississippi. Measles. First death in the camp. Attack on Holly Springs by the Rebels and capture and parole of the garrison. Pages 28-40.

CHAPTER IV.

March to Memphis. Foraging. Cooking beans. Ordered to Benton Barracks, St. Louis. In St. Louis. Back at home again. Exchange and ordered to front again. At New Madrid, Mo. At Columbus, guarding prisoners. Scouting in Kentucky and Tennessee. Sickness of men at Union City, Tenn. A raid in South-west Tennessee. A confederate citizen's strategy to prevent foraging. Return to Union City. Pages 41-51.

CHAPTER V.

Leave Union City. At Louisville. Proceed to Bridgeport, Ala. A rebel signal. Grant succeeds Rosecrans. Forward movement. Lookout Valley and Battle of Wauhatchie. Shelling from Lookout Mountain and casualites. Assault on Missionary Ridge and Lookout Mountain. Hooker's Battle above the clouds. Sherman's assault on Mission Ridge. Breaking the Rebel's center by Sheridan's and Wood's divisions. Grand victory of Union troops and route of the Confederates. Injury of the Author and conveyance to hospital. At Soldiers' Home in Chattanooga. "It was a piece of moole." Pages 52-69.

CHAPTER VI.

Safeguard in a Union man's home. Trying a Rebel gun. Return to the regiment at Kelly's

Ferry. Command returns to Bridgeport, Ala. Patroling. Capture of a Confederate. Affecting incident. Capture of a supposed Rebel city. By Corporal Moore and Author. Snowstorm and peach tree bloom. A Confederate's version of. Preparing for spring campaign of 1864. General Sherman in command. Resignation of officers. Appearance of Grand Army of Sherman. Pages 70-80.

CHAPTER VII.

The assault on the Confederate position at Dalton. Snake Creek Gap. Great victory at Resacca. General Hooker compliments the One Hundred and First Illinois. Pontoon bridges. Cross the Oustenaula river. Rebel desertions. Retreat of Confederates across Etawah river. Heavy battle at Pumpkin-vine creek. Great loss of the One Hundred and First Illinois. Fatalities. Death of our color bearer. The skirmish line. Cowardice. Peculiarities of wounded. Eccentric soldier. The confederate position on the Chattahoochie river. Sherman's strategy. The skeptical soldier. A presentiment of death. Battle of Peach Tree Creek. Mortal wound of the skeptic, and death. Confederate change of commanders. Siege of Atlanta. Experience of Author with sharp-shooters. Capture of sharp-shooters by the Yankees. Pages 81-98.

CHAPTER VIII.

Raising of the siege of Atlanta. The Twentieth corps position on the Chattahoochie. Elation of the Rebels at the supposed retreat of Sherman. Sherman surprises them at Jonesboro, thirty miles south of Atlanta. Union victory at Jonesboro. Evacuation of Atlanta. Occupation by the Twentieth corps and all the army and end of campaign. Confederate tactics to repair the disaster at Atlanta. Hood's rapid movements in the rear of Sherman's army. Battle of Altoona. Sherman's plan to checkmate Hood. The march to the sea planned. Destruction of Atlanta and grand march commenced. Uninterrupted progress of Sherman. The sweet potatoes, how they started from the ground. Foraging. Negroes starting for Massa Linkum. Pages 99-111.

CHAPTER IX.

Occupation of Milledgeville, the capital of Georgia. Consternation of the Confederates at Sherman's movement. Frantic appeals by the authorities of Rebeldom, to the people to resist Sherman. Grotesque appearance of the foragers. Kilpatrick's cavalry. The capture of Millen, but the prisoners removed. Destitute appearance of Millen. Some Rebel opposition. Approach to Savannah. Eating rice. Occupation of Savannah.

Flowers and mosquitoes in December. Pages 112-118.

CHAPTER X.

Leave Savannah. Difficulties of crossing the river by reason of floods. The campaign in South Carolina began. Sherman's adroit strategy perplexes the Confederates. Occupation of Columbia, S. C. Living off the country. The pine woods and the novelties of tar and turpentine production. General Sherman and mule-driver. Bad weather, bad roads. Corduroying. Bad economy of Rebels, destroying their own property. Occupation of Cheraw. Fayetteville. Foraging incidents. Battles of Bentonville and Averysboro. Occupation of Goldsboro and end of campaign. Pages 119-130.

CHAPTER XI.

Resting. Arrival of recruits. Fitting out for another campaign. Dejection of Confederates. Advance on Raleigh, N. C. Retreat of Rebel army. News of capture of Richmond and surrender of Lee's army. Lincoln's assassination. Truce with the Confederates. Final surrender of Johnston's army. March through Virginia. Richmond. March to Washington. Pages 131-140.

CHAPTER XII.

Arrival in Washington City. Grand review

and muster out of service. The journey homeward. Patriotic joy of the people. Hospitable reception at Lawrenceburg, Ind. Gov. Oglesby's care of Illinois soldiers. An unexpected banquet on the cars. Arrival at Springfield, Ills., and paid off. Arrival at Jacksonville and reception at home. Grand picnic dinner given to the One Hundred and First Illinois at Jacksonville, and final separation. Pages 141-156.

CHAPTERS XIII AND XIV.

Observations made in the South during a visit there in 1895. A soldier's memorial sermon preached at Montezuma, Iowa, May 26th, 1895. Pages 157-180.

Memorial Sermon, Pages 181-196.

Personal Reminiscences of the War.

CHAPTER I.

My first experience in military service was of a quasi character, obtained in the celebrated political campaign of the year 1860, when Mr. Lincoln was elected President. The slavery agitation was at fever heat, and the whole country was aroused. In the North, and especially in the State of Illinois, where I resided, there was great activity in both the great political parties, and marching clubs were formed. The Republican clubs were known as "Wide-Awakes." Their uniform consisted of an oil cloth cape and glazed cap. The marching was usually after night, and they carried lamps on long staffs, which, being carried in nearly an upright position, made a very brilliant display. These clubs paraded at all the rallies, and had much to do in awakening public sentiment and preparing the people for the great struggle that awaited them. The Democratic clubs also carried lamps, but their uniform differed from the Wide-Awakes, being capes and caps of hickory shirting, and their lamp staffs were of hickory wood, and they were known as Hickories, and were just as earnest and enthusiastic as the Wide-Awakes. Yet, a few months afterwards, when Fort Sumter was fired on and the great uprising of the loyal North occurred, the men and boys who had been known as Wide-Awakes and Hickories were in the main seized by the same patriotic fervor, and thousands of them, regardless of past political affiliations, fraternized as patriots and went into the Union army, and marched and fought side by side till the overthrow of the rebellion was accomplished.

I remember one incident connected with the political campaign preceding the outbreak of the war. Mr. Lincoln's home was in Springfield, Ills., and about Sept. 1, 1860, a monster rally was held there. The Wide-Awake clubs for miles around and thousands of other people attended. It was thought that more than one hundred thousand strangers were in Springfield, to see their favorite candidate and pay their respects, little thinking, however, that, even if elected, he would become the most notable President the country ever had, and whose fame would be world-wide and historic forever. But, not to digress too much, we had an Irishman in our club. His name was Mike O'Conner. He was unlike most of his nationality—he was a radical and enthusiastic Republican, and on this account was almost idolized by his comrades of the club. At his earnest solicitation the captain took the company to pay our respects to Mr. Lincoln, who, in his genial way, shook hands with every member. When he came to Mike, the latter spoke out and said: "Maester Lincoln, I am an Irishman, and a strong Rapublican, and it's not often ye see the likes o' me, sure!" Mr. Lincoln seemed much amused at his honest demeanor, and held his hand quite awhile, and assured him of his hearty appreciation that there was one of Erin's natives who would give him a loyal support. But poor Mike, he did not get to vote for his favorite. He was so earnest and active in the numerous rallies that the exertion and exposure brought on typhoid fever, and he died just three days before the election, greatly mourned by all his comrades.

The election being held, Mr. Lincoln was duly elected. The Republicans, of course, were jubilant. But the South soon began to show their hostility, and before the inauguration took place South Carolina and five other states seceded, and ominous war clouds hovered over the country. The winter of 1860 and 1861 was a very unsettled period, yet it was hard for the North to realize that the South meant to carry out the threats of disunion. I remember the most startling sensation I experienced was at a lyceum, when one of the speakers, an ultra-Democrat, sneeringly referred to the Wide-Awakes, and wondered if they would be as keen to fight for Abe Lincoln as they were to march before the election. The remark stung me to the quick, but I said nothing, and was much horrified at the thought of war. This man, however, went into the Union army before I did, and, as I learned since the war, lost his life in the battle of Shiloh.

In the autumn of 1861, it having been settled that the "unpleasantness" would be more than a "breakfast spell," but a continued and desperate struggle that might last several years—the President's call for troops already was up in the hundreds of thousands—I felt impelled to enlist. I had barely reached my eighteenth year, and, not acquainting my parents with my design, I enlisted in a military company, that afterwards became Co. F, 33d Illinois Infantry. My father, when he heard of it, was much opposed to what I had done, but said little to me; he went right away, and before muster in had my name stricken from the company roll, which, at that time, was allowable. The war raged for another year. Fort Donalson, Shiloh and other battles had been fought, with varying results. All this time I was restive, and was so anxious for the success of the Union cause I longed for the seat of war--not that I wanted to fight or riot in the carnage of battle, for I still had a dread of the clash of arms, that, even now, I cannot reconcile with my great desire to go to war; but I thought it was as much my duty as any one's to try and save the country. So, when the news came of the sanguinary and disappointing results of McClellan's peninsular campaign, coupled with the President's call for six hundred thousand more men, I urged my parents to consent to my enlistment, which was reluctantly given. I remember that one of the arguments used was that, in event of the State's quota not being filled, drafting would be resorted to, and that probably drafted men would not fare so well, and I or a younger brother would likely be compelled to go. Whether this was the clincher that procured parental consent I can hardly say, but on the afternoon of Aug. 6, 1862, a boon companion and I went to the county seat, where recruiting was actively going on, and enlisted for three years, or during the war; that is, if the war closed before the three years was up, the government could discharge us.

The company was being rapidly filled. Mr. J. T. Newman, who had been an active business man and was quite well respected in Jacksonville, Ill., was the principal man in raising this company, and of course it was understood that he would be the Captain. He, however, was elected Major when the regiment was organized, and John A. Lightfoot was commissioned the first Captain; F. E. Shafer, First Lieutenant; T. M. Guy, Second Lieutenant. The company had the full complement of one hundred and one men. Nine other companies were raised in the county and formed the regiment, and before muster in to the United States service and numbered it was known as the Morgan County regiment. Being sworn into the State service, we were full-fledged soldiers, in respect to obeying orders and leaving home and civil pursuits were concerned, and in a very few days we were in camp, on the county fair grounds, which was known as Camp Duncan, so named after one of the Governors of Illinois, whose widow and family lived on a contiguous lot. We were soon made familiar with military routine, as roll call, company, squad and batallion drill and guard duty. A number of men who had gone out in the first call of three months service re-enlisted. They seemed to us raw levies very expert in drill and other military matters. They were given mostly the non-commissioned offices, as Sergeants, Corporals, etc. These usually had charge of the daily drill exercise, and in a little time we imagined ourselves proficient in executing all the scientific features of "Hardee's Light Infantry Tactics."

We were a proud set of boys when we drew our first uniforms and guns and equipages. I remember, however, how clumsy I felt with knapsack, cartridge box, haversack and canteen strapped on, with the old Belgian musket, the whole business weighing from fifty to seventy-five pounds. I had been used to farm in summer time, going in my shirt sleeves, or in winter time swinging the ax, without encumbrance. I felt almost as much hampered as a young colt hitched to an old stand-by horse and a farm wagon for the first time. In fact, I did not see how I could carry all that toggery and make much headway in breaking the backbone of the rebellion, or any other bone, for that matter. I was quite discouraged, and if I could have found any physical blemish sufficient for rejection I believe I would have been glad to have gone back to the farm and let my patriotism spend itself in sympathy and good wishes for the Union cause.

CHAPTER II.

On the second of September the regiment was mustered into the United States service by a regular army officer, and numbered the One Hundred and First Illinois Infantry. Our company was made Co. I, and C. H. Fox, a lawyer of Jacksonville, was elected and commissioned Colonel; W. J. Wyatt, of Franklin, who had seen service in the Mexican war, was commissioned Lieut. Colonel, and, as before stated, J. T. Newman became Major. From the 2d of September to October 6th we remained at Camp Duncan, getting all the military instruction we could. The people of Jacksonville and Morgan County seemed very much interested in us, and every day the camp was thronged with visitors. Our fathers, mothers, brothers, sisters and sweethearts (for nearly "every laddie had his lassie"), and many other loyal people would come to see how we fared as soldiers and witness the company and batallion drill. They frequently brought baskets laden with the abundant provisions and delicacies of the farm. Sympathizing mothers were lavish in these kind attentions to their brave sons, who they realized would soon be far from the paternal roof and engaged in awful warfare to save the Union.

These were pleasant days to all, but soon the order came to embark for the seat of war. It was one Monday morning when marching orders came. The men had nearly all received passes to spend the Sabbath at their homes, and were scattered all over the county, but, as far as known to me, all came in time to catch the train. Friends and relatives also came to bid good-bye and see the boys safely off. Perhaps it will never fall to my lot to see again such a melting scene. A thousand men, from nearly as many homes, departing on the perilous enterprise of war, which had already made desolate many homes. Of course some of these brave lads would not return, but who they were none could tell. These thoughts flitted through many minds, and all, perhaps, partook more or less of the gloom fostered by them. As mother, sister and lover embraced the object of their affection there would be the misgiving that perhaps I may never see him again, and our home, too, will have a "vacant chair." Many wept profusely and seemed almost without consolation as the horrors of war were vividly depicted upon the imagination. At last the locomotive gave a shrill whistle and the bell began to ring. The boys seated themselves in the cars, friends spoke their last adieus, and we were soon speeding away toward the enemy's country.

After any great tension of feeling it is natural there should be a reaction, yet I was surprised to notice that those who had indicated the greatest emotion and wept the most profusely were the first to assume cheerfulness and commence to laugh and joke, as if they were going on a mere pleasure trip for a short time, instead of a three years' tussle with "grim-visaged war;" while others who had evidenced no emotion began to assume painful expression of countenance, and look as dejected as though they had lost every friend they had. My theory is, tears are a blessed relief to those whose grief finds vent in them; they are soonest consoled, and sad memories are easier forgotten. Not so with those who cannot cry; their agonies are pent up, and gnaw upon their feelings, perhaps for days and weeks, before they emerge from their power.

A night and a day we rode away, and at sundown we reached our destination, Cairo, at the confluence of the Ohio and Mississippi rivers; after debarking from the train we fell into line and marched to a parade ground below the city. Cairo had early been occupied as a point of military importance, and the citizens were used to the coming and going of troops, and did not seem particularly impressed by the fact of a thousand armed men moving through their streets, and what seemed strange to me, no man or woman, or even small boy, asked a word about us. Monitors and gunboats were anchored in the river, many fine transports were at the wharves, and many naval and military officers and men passed to and fro, yet no one said "Howd'ye do?" or "Where are you from?" so that it seemed to me a cold reception which was extended to us.

When we halted on that well-worn parade ground we hardly knew what the order would be, but soon got orders to stack arms by companies, break ranks and cook our suppers. We had no chance to cook on the train, so it took no second hint to go to work and provide the usual soldiers' repast of coffee and hard tack, with a slice of bacon sandwiched in between, and soon all were busy. My name was called for guard duty, to report right away, and I had to leave the almost prepared meal with my messmates, and satisfy my hunger from a few scraps that remained in my haversack, and drink water from the river, instead of coffee. That night I was so tired and sleepy I did not see how I could keep awake the two hours I should be on post, for we had already learned that death was the penalty to a sentinel found sleeping on duty, so it was a matter of vital concern to me to obviate in some way the spell of drowsiness upon me. I soon hit upon a happy expedient to promote wakefulness. Cairo was then terribly infested with rats, which were nearly always visible and running in every direction. I conceived them to be enemies which should be put to the sword, or bayonet, rather, so I sought to pin them to the earth with that weapon; they seemed, however, quite expert in avoiding my thrusts, so that I had no victims, but my point was gained—the two hours glided rapidly away, and by the next relief I was sufficiently rested to perform my duty without getting drowsy.

The next day we occupied the barracks that had been vacated by a regiment which went down the river; they were rude, but comfortable structures and we were permitted to enjoy them until November 26th, when we, too, went down into Dixie. Our chief employment was fatigue duty and guarding prisoners; these were a motley-looking set, with nearly every variety of garb, the butternut jeans and Confederate regulation gray prevailing somewhat, as a semblance of uniform, but so threadbare as to furnish but feeble protection from the chilly November blast. The latest arrivals were from the battle of Perryville, and some were a part of the Fort Donelson capture. Some of them were very talkative, and in eloquent style defended the Confederacy. I never found one who would admit that we should finally succeed in whipping them, their staple arguments being, that "Cotton was King," and that we could never subjugate a brave people like they were. There was no attempt made to escape, though the barracks they occupied were slender structures, and we being still raw and inexperienced might easily have been imposed upon and outwitted. It seems to me they were more intent upon drawing Uncle Sam's rations, especially the coffee, than projecting an escape, the result of which would be to be thrust into battle again. They had smelled some powder, and I judged that if they were fed well and allowed to talk freely they would esteem the Union prison a more healthy location than to be with Bragg's legions in the battle front. They seemed to while away the time by killing "graybacks," of which they had a good supply, and whittling rings out of muscle shells, bone, wood, and other substances of sufficient durability for the purpose. The weather a great deal of the time was rainy, and guard duty was very unpleasant; many of the boys contracted colds and became quite sick, some were sent to the hospital, some of whom never saw any active service afterwards.

The hardier class of men kept in good cheer,

and the time that they were off duty was spent in washing and mending their clothes, reading, writing to friends, playing cards, and frequently playing practical jokes upon each other. Sometimes a private soldier would forget his place and crack a joke at the expense of his superiors, the officers; indeed, the tendency to mirthfulness was such that time and place were ignored, and the love of fun bore down all restraint. One morning at guard mounting, which in camp is always conducted in regulation order, the column was standing at "parade rest." The Colonel, in full uniform and gay sash, mounted on his fine charger, which was feeling his oats quite well, saw the colors fluttering, and got scared, and reared and plunged, becoming almost umanageable; one of the wags, seeing the Colonel's predicament, crudely called out, "Pull the strings, Colonel," and all the men, struck by the ludicrousness of the affair, were convulsed with laughter, which the Colonel heard with deep chagrin. He soon brought the animal under control, and riding up to the Sergeant-Major, asked who the man was that dared to hollow at him. That officer respectfully saluted, and replied that he did not know. "Well," said the Colonel, "you find out and I'll send him to the guard-house." The Sergeant-Major went from the head to the foot of the column and inquired of every man, and strange enough, every one said they did not know. When the indignant Colonel learned the result of the inquiry he was livid with rage, said something about a pack of liars, and rode away.

One of the jokers picked up an old rusty bridle bit and went to the sutler's tent to buy cigars. Now, at that time silver coin was nearly all out of circulation, but a few stray pieces would turn up now and then; twelve and one-half cents, in western parlance, was called a bit, and some of them were still out, but they were rare. When the wag reached the counter he asked if they would sell him a bit's worth of cigars. The obliging clerk said yes, and laid out three which were eagerly seized by the purchaser, the old rusty bit was laid on the counter to pay for them, and the boy, with a loud guffaw, speedily retired to his quarters.

CHAPTER III.

When the orders came for us to leave Cairo we were to travel by water and go down the Mississippi—no one in the ranks seemed to know or care, so we got away from there. By 10 o'clock a. m., November 26th, all were aboard the steamer Universe, and soon with her precious freight she was steaming down the river. It was a beautiful day for the time of year, and patriotic emotions seemed to stir every soul, as we felt we were nearing the scene of actual conflict. A singing club, composed, I believe, of members of Company G, collected on the hurricane deck, in front of the smoke stacks, and sang patriotic airs, some of them new to me. They sung "Rally 'Round the Flag, Boys," with unusual fervor, and as it was the first time I had heard that noble song I was greatly enthused by it. Soon we were nearing Columbus, the late rebel stronghold, on one side of the river, and the Belmont battlefield on the other, every eye being strained to catch a view of those historic land-marks, and, to our surprise, the prow of the boat headed to the Kentucky shore, and we were soon engaged in the bustle of debarkation. There we were to board the cars on the Mobile & Ohio Railway for the immediate front. At Cairo we had shipped our regimental teams and ambulance. Our company teamster had taken sick and was sent to Mound City Hospital, and I was temporarily detailed to fill his place till he should return to the regiment. He never did return, and I never knew what became of him. However, I had double responsibility thrust on me, for I still retained my gun and accoutrements, and had a team of two horses and a wagon, and to see to their being loaded and unloaded on steamboat or cars, as the case might be.

When we came to load on the cars at Columbus the men occupied all available space, inside and outside, of the common box cars that had been provided, so there was no room for horses or wagons. The wagonmaster was hurried off as quartermaster's assistant, to meet emergencies at the front, and a half-dozen of us, with the teams, were left, temporarily, till we could be shipped forward. We expected to go in a day or two, but it was two weeks before we could secure transportation. Up to this time I had been able to keep myself in respectable attire, and washed my clothes and changed every week. When my lot was cast with a different set of men things were decidedly changed, and my later companions were not inclined to be as particular as my own company boys were. Then we were quartered on an old rebel camp, and actually occupied a shanty they had used. I began to suspect that an invasion had actually taken place upon my most private rights, namely, the "pediculus" entrenching themselves in the nether garment. Like the girl with her first beau, I was ashamed to speak of their tender embraces, though I had reason to suspect my comrades of a like experience and perhaps dating farther back than mine. But I resolved on reconnoitering the situation. Outside of the town limits there was a skirt of forest trees, and I told my comrades I believed there might be found some persimmons, as I knew they were indigenous to the "dark and bloody ground." They laughed me to scorn. This suited me, as I did not crave their company in my proposed search for them. They tried to scare me out of my project by saying the Johnnies would get me, for we were in their country now. Nothing daunted, however, I went to the woods, being careful not to go beyond the picket line, and, sure enough, I found persimmons, plenty of them, and enjoyed eating them very much. I took a good supply to camp, and ignoring their raillery in the morning, I gave the boys what I brought in. I did not reveal to them the discovery that affected me the most—that when sufficiently obscured from view, I slipped outside my shirt, and proceeded to interview my nearest neighbors and call a halt to their pretensions. I judge my emotions were slightly different from Balboa, when he discovered the Pacific Ocean from a mountain peak in Panama; for I was not at all elated by my discovery, and murderously exterminated the invaders of my personal estate. After I had vanquished them I returned to camp, no one suspecting the chief object of my morning walk.

The officer who had charge of railway transportation came the morning of Dec. 10th, and told us he could send us forward that day. There was some danger of the rebels raiding the road, but we would have to take the risk. Several cars of horses and a lot of contrabands were to go. The horses would of course have to be put inside the cars, as the rolling stock was limited. The contrabands and ourselves would have to ride on the outside. I did not take kindly to that method of travel, as part of the trip would have to be taken in the night and I feared for my personal safety, but at Columbus the wagonmaster gave me charge of the ambulance, a covered vehicle, with springs, to carry the sick and wounded soldiers. It was loaded on a flat and made secure, so at night one of the boys and I slept in it. At Grand Junction there was an alarm raised of rebels threatening the road, so we were detained for the night. The troops there were kept under arms all night, in case of an attack. A flat car had been barricaded and two cannon mounted on it. The artillerymen were old veterans and seemed to enjoy the prospect for a fight, so they could try their guns from their fort on wheels, as they called it. It was a bitter cold night. My chum and I were compelled to leave our bed in the ambulance and go to a large, blazing fire near by, that the battery boys kept feeding with good, fine lumber, as there were thousands of feet stacked up in a lumber yard close by. I enjoyed the warmth of the fire, but my nature revolted at the wasteful destruction of such valuable lumber. The battery boys were very kind to us. Our rations were rather scant, and they gave us a supply of hard bread, of which they seemed to have no lack. We boiled a kettle of coffee, and were told to make ourselves welcome to their fire and not freeze to death on the cars. We were pleased to share their kind hospitality; but some colored men who had come in to escape the toils of bondage did not fare so well. I never could understand the antipathy of some white men towards the colored race; their detestation of them, on account of color, and their delight in torturing them. Our hosts were men of this type. They were lavish in their kindness to us, but cruel to the unfortunate men of color. These poor runaways begged to stop and warm at the roaring fire. They were told rudely they might warm awhile, and soon depart, for they did not want them there. The poor men sank down by the fire, and, seeming in a very exhausted state, were soon snoring, fast asleep. Soon one of the battery men, annoyed by the loud snoring, said: "Look at them niggers, gone fast asleep! They said they'd go directly, and they've taken up quarters for the night. Come, boys, let's cook them!" and, to my great horror, proceeded to drag the negroes through the blazing fire. I could hardly reconcile their cruelty to them to the great kindness they had shown us. Can the casuist explain how such a streak of the milk of human kindness and such a display of ferocious cruelty unite in one breast? Thus I was touched on two sides of my nature, but was powerless to obviate the cruelty shown the colored men because we had been the recipients of great favors at the hands of the offenders, and all parties were entire strangers to us. Truly the phenomena of human nature is the greatest mystery of the universe.

The next morning the locomotive hooked onto our train, and after many delays at the different stations we finally reached Holly Springs, Miss. The regiment had been assigned to a brigade and division, and for a few days were at the front in Grant's first movement on Vicksburg. For some reason they were detached and sent back to Holly Springs, to do provost and guard duty there, where we found them. Though not all in town, several companies occupied block houses on the railroad, north to near Cold Water Station. Company G was sent back to the city soon after we came there. The measles broke out, and most of the boys who had not had them were down sick. I was in charge of a regimental ambulance, and took several loads of sick to the hospital. Some of them never recovered, and were buried without coffins in that far-off Southland. Our company lost a man by the name of Henry Fresher. He was an awkward mortal. No music whatever in him. He could not keep the step in drill, and the officers vainly tried to have him overcome this defect, so he became the butt of many a joke by his waggish comrades. He was no doubt as patriotic as any of us, and honest in the performance of his duty, and deplored his misfortune, but of course he could not help it. He felt keenly the disparaging remarks made about him, yet I never heard him complain. When we wrapped him in his blanket and lowered him in the cold grave, without ceremony, save the usual military salute, several of the boys broke down entirely, and tears chased down their cheeks freely. I heard one of them say: "Well, we were too hard on Fresher, and I'll never make fun of any man again about what he cannot help," his conscience perhaps troubling him about it.

Holly Springs is in the midst of the cotton-growing region, and speculators, despite the orders of Gen. Grant, were buying and collecting all they could. I rather suspect some of the army officers were also involved; anyway, great quantities had accumulated, and it was being brought in more or less every day. The country was full of forage and provisions of every kind, and we were faring too sumptuously for it to continue. As far as I was concerned, I had a feeling of security, similar to that I enjoyed before leaving my Illinois home, when suddenly, at early dawn, on the 20th of December, 1862, we were startled by the noted rebel yell and the rapid discharge of hundreds of firearms near the depot, perhaps three-quarters of a mile from our corral. We were quartered in part of a dwelling house, by permission of the residents, they thinking we would protect them from the depredations of our men who might be disposed to foraging. I was acting as cook that morning, and had my sleeves rolled up and hands in dough, making biscuit. I could scarcely think we were attacked, and, hearing some confusion in the street, I just stepped out of doors, when behold! the whole street was full of mounted rebels, and seemingly all over the town, and not an armed force of ours visible anywhere. I had gone too far to retreat; in fact, if I had dodged back into the house it would not have availed anything, for we were securely bagged. We each of us retained our muskets, but, because we were teamsters, no cartridges had been issued to us. We could neither fight nor run. As soon as they caught a glimpse of me, several shots were fired, but, providentially, I was unharmed. An officer, seeing I was completely at their mercy, prevented any more firing at me, and I became a prisoner of war. As soon as the true state of affairs was known, they let me return into the house to secure my overcoat and knapsack, a guard going with me. He reported seeing guns in one corner of the room, with the cartridge boxes. Some of the rebels went in and brought them out, breaking them to pieces, but, not finding any cartridges, they asked for them. I told them that we, being in charge of the teams, never had any, at which they laughed immoderately, and started us double-quick to the depot, which was their temporary headquarters. Here we found the commander of the post, Col. Murphy; Col. Fox, of our regiment, and four companies of the 101st all prisoners, with some of the 2d Illinois Cavalry and 26th Illinois Infantry. In an hour or two Company I, which had fought them for a while, but was overpowered with great numbers, was also brought in. This was a very disgraceful surrender on the part of Col. Murphy, who, if not untrue to the cause, was too much of an imbecile to command troops in time of action. Gen. Grant, in his Memoirs, fully exonerates all the men, but blames Murphy for all the disaster, and had him cashiered from the service. The men afterwards redeemed themselves in numerous skirmishes and battles in which they were engaged. Our captors were some of them disposed to be harsh in their treatment of us, part of them taking the personal effects of a portion of their captives. They had an ardent desire to secure our overcoats, as they were almost entirely new, many of them not having any, and it was easy to dye them and change them from the sky-blue to any color they desired. One awkward looking man, with revolver pointed at me, demanded I should take off my overcoat. I looked him steadily in the eye, and I judged he was not mean enough to shoot me if I resisted. I felt sure he wilted under my gaze, so I remarked I could not spare my coat. I did not know what they would do with us and where we should go. It was winter time, and if I had to die I believed I would as soon be shot as to perish with cold. I was pleased to see him put up his pistol and ride away. Later in the day they found our quartermaster's stores. They secured clothing of every kind, more than they could carry on their horses, and some of them actually divided their spoils with the prisoners. I secured a pair of shoes and socks, which I was sadly in need of, and, under the circumstances, felt somewhat grateful.

It was impossible to get us away to their lines, so we were paroled. It took about all day to go through this process, and a little before nightfall they left us where they found us, but in great humiliation at what had occurred. That night was a scene of anarchy and destruction. The Rebels had fired the cotton and all buildings in which was kept government stores, and the town was burning up. No one seemed to care much, soldiers, citizens and negroes, all seemed bent on securing what plunder they could. Stores and dwellings not burning were searched; some looking for money, some for something to drink, and some for whatever they could find that could be carried off and be of some use. Some of our men, in their mad thirst for drink, went through a drug store, and in spite of the entreaties of the more sober minded, insisted on tasting everything in bottles, and two or three were poisoned. John Almon died a most horrible death, suffering the most excruciating agony before he passed away. Several came pretty near the same fate, and one, S. C. Groves, became entirely insane and was lost. It was never known what became of him, but it is thought that some of the Rebel citizens put him out of the way for fear of his insanity. Surely, that night was a terror. The loss of private property was so great that it was no benefit to the citizens of Holly Springs, altho' most of them were jubilant because the Yankees had been captured. The surrender included about half the regiment, only, companies A, D, G, H and K, with their officers escaped by falling back to Coldwater and formed a junction with the forces there, repelled the assault on that place. Most of these men saw hard service on what was called the mosquito fleet, and ran the blockade at Vicksburg and were granted a thirty day furlough as a reward for that service. The field officers were all taken, which led many to believe that the entire regiment had been captured, so that we were often twitted by the veterans as being green, and as they thought, too easily taken in. But as Gen. Grant attaches all blame and responsibility to Col. Murphy, of the 8th Wisconsin, the regiment that carried "Old Abe," the eagle, through the war, it is an injustice to the 101st Illinois to charge them with cowardice or inefficiency in the matter. It was not till nearly noon of the following day that the advance guard of Grant's army reached Holly Springs and took in the deplorable situation. This successful raid of the Rebels compelled the falling back of the entire army to Memphis, and prevented Grant's co-opperation with Sherman on the contemplated assault on Vicksburg. Sherman moved without knowing what had befallen Grant's communication or his retreat, and was badly repulsed at Chickasaw, near Vicksburg, and was compelled to retire. It was a sad string of disastrous results, brought about by the cowardice or inefficiency of the post commander of Holly Springs.

CHAPTER IV.

In a few days we took up our line of march to Memphis, which was about forty-five miles northwest. Having lost our supplies at Holly Springs we received orders to forage liberally off the country, which was rich in all kinds of provisions, so that we lived on the fat of the land. My mess had four men in it. One night we reached camp loaded down with sweet potatoes, bacon, corn meal, sugar and a large fat goose. Of course our meals were prepared with Jeffersonian simplicity to suit the occasion of haste and lack of cooking apparatus, with limited experience in culinary matters. The potatoes were roasted in the ashes, as was also the goose, that was crudely preserved by taking out the entrails and cutting off the head and feet, covering it with ashes and hot coals the feathers burned to a crisp, and when it was thought to be done it was taken out and the crisp formation peeled off slick as an onion, and it was fairly well cooked, and furnished an enjoyable meal. The next afternoon we reached Memphis, but remained only a few days. Here a practical joke was played on one of our men. He was a man of large physical proportions and vigorous constitution, and withal a tremendous appetite; so much so that no one could afford to mess with him and hold their share of rations; so he usually drew his separately, and cooked and ate alone. One day he prepared a mess of beans. With indefatigable labor he carried wood from a drift on a sand bar more than a half a mile away, fuel not being supplied as we were soon to leave. He early put on a medium sized camp kettle, and it was nearly full and well cooked when he took it off the fire and set it by his tent door, covering it with a tin plate, and went in. One of the boys who had been watching him seized the kettle and took it into an adjoining tent and quickly poured the beans into a couple of mess pans. He then set the kettle back where he found it, covering it with the plate as it was. Sandy, as he was called, passed in and out two or three times, yet had not missed the beans, while the boys in the other tent had time to stow them all away in their hungry stomachs. Finally he concluded to eat his dinner, and uncovered the kettle, when, to his surprise, they had all disappeared. Of course the guilty parties were ready to denounce the thief, and surmise probabilities. When the actual thief declared he had seen two suspicious looking negroes slipping through the camp, Sandy caught on right away and cursed the whole fraternity of

Contrabands, and old Abe Lincoln for setting them free, while the bad boys chuckled in their sleeves. Sandy, however, was not going to do without his meal, so he made another weary trip to the driftwood, put on another kettle of beans, and by four o'clock p. m. partook of a nourishing repast.

On the 1st of January, all the men who could satisfy the authorities that they were actually paroled, were ordered to Benton Barracks, St. Louis. The boat we were on had sustained an injury, and could make but poor headway up stream; sometimes the current was so strong she was turned round by the force of it; twice we were grounded on sand bars, and the second time we were put in another boat that came along that made better time, and succeeded in getting us to Cairo, where we were put on shore and awaited the arrival of the boat that was chartered to take us to St. Louis. Next day she came in and we were glad to get aboard again as it was not very comfortable camping out that season of the year. The ninth day after leaving Memphis we reached our destination. I had never been in St. Louis before, nor seen Barracks on such an extensive scale, and was much impressed by what I saw; some of the boys took special delight in reading the signs out loud as we passed through the business part of the city. It must have sounded very ludicrous to the citizens to hear more than a dozen boys read the restaurant signs, hot coffee, pies and cakes, cheese and crackers, and pickled pigs feet, etc·, etc., over, and over again, till it became the most stupid of bores to the more discreet and orderly men of the Battalion.

We were assigned very comfortable quarters, rations were abundant and nothing to do. The commander of the post, I think, expected us to do fatigue duty, and stand guard with a short club, and obey other orders which we construed to be a violation of the parole, which was explicit in stating that we were not to do any military duty whatever until regularly exchangad. It was right for the government to furnish barracks, rations and transportation for us, but not exact duty of a military character, our conscientious scruples were respected, and we learned, somehow, if we took a French furlough to our homes we would not be regarded as deserters, so nearly all left for their homes. It was about a hundred miles north to Morgan county, Illinois, and about the first of February I was back in the land of peace and plenty, not very proud of my military record up to this date. I think perhaps our friends at home were nearly as much humiliated as ourselves. I remember calling to mind the old couplet, "The king of France, with forty thousand men, marched up a hill, and then marched back again." Our short, humiliating military experience suggested the same innocuous outcome. We were careful to be at the barracks when it was time to muster for pay, which was every two months. The days of our pleasant captivity continued about six months when an exchange of prisoners was effected. It afforded a good opportunity for desertion to those who had lost heart in the cause or were tired of the service, but it is creditable to state that not more than a dozen failed to return when notified by the government of exchange. About the middle of June we were ready to march to the front, and again we were floating on the bosom of the "Father of Waters," bound for the enemy's country. We thought we should go directly to Vicksburg, which, at this time was vigorously besieged by Grant's army, but we were landed at New Madrid, Mo. I remembered reading in my schoolboy days, of a destructive earthquake there in 1811, so the place was historic to me from this, and the fact of Gen. Pope's brilliant operations here the year before. Here we found the 23d Missouri Infantry and a batallion of the 4th Missouri Cavalry, with which we were brigaded and, I think, formed a part of the 16th army corps, but we never saw the rest of that command till Sherman began the Atlanta campaign, nearly a year later, then we had become a part of the Army of the Cumberland.

After the surrender of Vicksburg we were sent up the river to Columbus, and for two or three weeks guarded prisoners there. These were a desperate set of men, and gave us much trouble. A rebel force was supposed to be hovering near, and nearly every night there was an alarm given and the long roll beat, and we would frequently be under arms all night. The frequency of these made it tiresome, yet we cheerfully put up with it, as a matter of discipline, for none of us wanted a repetition of the Holly Springs experience. We finally were ordered to advance into the interior and scatter the enemy if any should be found. We compassed a good deal of territory, marched some hundreds of miles, visited several towns in Kentucky and Tennessee, but we never saw any armed rebels, though we deployed several times.

Near the town of Mayfield was a large tobacco factory, and much of the weed was there in store, and no doubt a good deal of it found its way to the rebel army. As we were two or three days in this neighborhood, some of the tobacco mysteriously disappeared. The owner made complaint to the brigade commander that his men had taken it and he wanted satisfaction. He was told that a search would be made, and if tobacco was found in the camp it should be restored and the guilty parties punished. To our surprise a dress parade was called at 4 p. m. Now, we had not had a dress parade for so long we did not know what it meant, but when the adjutant read orders he announced that a search for tobacco would be instituted next morning, and in whose tent it was found they would be held guilty of theft and summarily dealt with. Some of the boys said they saw the old colonel "wink the other eye." Of course, while the search was very thorough, there was not a plug to be found. Shortly after noon the old gentleman came to see how matters stood. The colonel pretended to be greatly enraged that his brave men should be charged with such a crime, as he had fully attested their innocence and told the old man if he had lost any tobacco his own dirty niggers had stolen it. "You now get away from here quick or I'll put you under arrest," and the old man retired, very much crestfallen.

We had in our mess a man who went by the name of Bob who had an inordinate taste for sweet things. He never could get enough sugar. The army ration was entirely inadequate for his need, hence he was begging, buying or stealing it almost continually. In one of our camping places was found a variety of sand, a good fac simile of the sugar of those times. Jule, another messmate, brought a tin cup full of it and placed it on our humble board at dinner, all being in the secret except Bob, for whom it was designed. He poured out his coffee, and, with a large table spoon, he made a dive into the supposed sugar. One heaping spoonful was energetically stirred in, when he tasted, but it was not sweet. The second and third spoon, fuller than before, found their way into the smoking beverage, when, thinking it very strange it did not sweeten, he took a pinch, in thumb and finger, and inserted it in his opening maw, when he began to spit and sputter, to eject it from his mouth. Then Jule, in great indignation, remarked: "Bob, you great hog, I brought that sand up to scour my gun, and you have nearly wasted it all trying to sweeten your coffee with it." Bob innocently remarked he was very sorry; he thought it was sugar, when all the boys just roared with laughter.

About the middle of August we went into camp at Union City, Tenn., a small village, but a good farming country round about. The weather was intensely hot, and it seemed unhealthy as many were taken with dysentery and diarrhœa, some cases becoming chronic, and compelling some to go to the hospital. I was taken down and reported to the regimental surgeon, who gave me some medicine and excused me from duty. About a week I was unable to do anything, but, recovering sufficiently, I returned to duty. This was the only time I ever received a prescription from a surgeon during my service, tho' many times feeling quite unwell, and never fully recovering from that attack, and have had frequent and painful recurrence of the disease ever since. In the last half of September a raiding expedition was sent to move in a south-east direction, to move light and to forage off the country. It was a region much infested with guerillas, and the people intensely disloyal. We were enable to discover any armed force, but picked up a few Confederates that were on furlough or deserters. As we were an infantry regiment, we could not keep pace with the cavalry that formed a part of the command, so the commander ordered us to seize horses and mount ourselves, for the country was quite well supplied with them. I think in less than two days every man was mounted, either on a horse or a mule, and we moved very rapidly and scoured the country in every direction. The plantations, many of them, were large, with good orchards and plenty of stock and provisions, so that we were in no danger of starving. Indeed, we became more and more emboldened to live off the enemy's country, and compelled them to furnish abundant support, which they did grudgingly. Our method, when near meal-time, would be to separate by companies and each go to a plantation and demand entertainment for thirty or forty men, as the case might be. Consternation was frequently depicted on the countenances of our hosts, but for fear we might levy even a heavier tribute than that, they acquiesced with the best grace possible. One evening we came to a large plantation with a double log house and customary veranda in front, and were waiting the preparation of the meal by the colored servants, two daughters of our host directing the same. The old gentleman thought, by artifice, to rid himself of his unwelcome company. He stepped up to the lieutenant in command and said: "Capting, I am 'fraid youans is running a great risk stopping here so long. This mornin' about five hundred of our men went past heah, and said likely they'd be back agin night. As there isn't more 'an thirty o' youans, they'd be sure to take youans in." The lieutenant looked serious and said: "Is that so?" "Yes," said the old man, "I'm looking for them every minute." Our commander was a native of Prussia, but spoke English fluently, and was not to be bluffed so easily. He took a musket and began to punch the chinking out between the logs of the house. The old man immediately asked why he did so. "Oh," said the lieutenant, "if those friends of yours come we want to prepare to meet them." "Good God, Capting, youans wouldn't fight right here in the house, would ye?" "Why, yes, this is the place, and if there are five hundred of your men, you see, shooting between the logs, we could soon kill them all, and they could not touch one of us in here. Of course, this is the very place to fight them." The old man came to a full stop and cut his quid very fine, and finally drawled out: "Well, Capting, it's a mistake about the Confederates bein' any whar's 'bout heah. I haven't seen any for more 'an a month." The boys broke out in a loud laugh, and the lieutenant ceased from his hostile demonstrations and quietly sat down and waited until the meal was ready. The conversation, on the part of the old gentleman, lagged after this, and pretty soon the meal was dispatched and we rode rapidly away, leaving our hosts to congratulate themselves on the great honor of entertaining a squad of hated Yankees. We picked up a great many horses and mules, and took off the country the means of our subsistence, but did not destroy anything we did not want, and left them in peaceful possession of their goods. We found some peach brandy and apple jack, the favorite drinks of the country, which they were loath to part with. We were usually satisfied with small quantities of this, and always left them the "lion's share" of that commodity, for we did not want to take on more than we could carry well.

CHAPTER V.

In the midst of this picnic affair, a courier from Union City came in great haste and said orders had come for our immediate departure for the scene of operations, near Chattanooga, and also informed us that Gen'l Rosecrans had been badly defeated at Chicamauga. By hard riding we reached Union City about 4 p. m., where we turned over our captures and struck tents, packed our knapsacks and boarded the train for Columbus. In a few hours we were at that point, embarked on a steamboat, and started up the river to Cairo. Here we took the cars again and proceeded north, and for awhile we were at a loss to know what was going to happen us. Some inventive genius started the report that, since our exchange, we had rendered such valuable service we were going to be treated to a thirty-day furlough and sent home to enjoy it. I had no hopes of such a favor, yet some of the boys hugged it as a delusive phantom of hope till we were switched onto a railway running east and left our own fair state, entering Indiana at Vincennes, when their pleasing dream subsided. Next morning we arrived at New

Albany, left the cars, crossed the river, and trod the sacred soil of old Kentucky once more. A short march brought us to Louisville, where, on account of the number of reinforcements going from the Army of the Potomac to Rosecrans, we were delayed two or three days. By the first of October we reached Bridgeport, Alabama, where we went into camp and awaited further developments. For several weeks we were employed on fortifications, and made the position as strong as possible, for the rebels were supposed to be anxious to follow up the advantage they had secured by their victory at Chicamauga. We did not know till afterwards of the destitution of our forces in and around Chattanooga, but it was terrible, and Bragg thought it only a question of a very short time when Rosecrans would have to surrender. By thus waiting they lost what advantage there was obtained at Chicamauga, and it became to them a very barren victory. Our far-seeing generals soon formed such powerful combinations that they were able to assume again the offensive and wipe out the stain of Chicamauga, which was the only great battle where the western troops met with actual reverse.

This region is very mountainous, and a large mountain was opposite Bridgeport, on which were evidences of reconnoitering parties of the enemy.

The morning star used to come up from behind this mountain, and, as it rose above the horizon, seemed quite large for a star. As it appeared to glimmer among the tree tops, it was sometimes taken for a rebel signal light. A story is told of an artillery officer, being exasperated at the thought of such effrontery of the rebels displaying a signal so close, that he ordered his battery to throw a shell into the impudent fellows. The sergeant, whose knowledge of astronomy was more profound than his superior, ventured to remark it was not a rebel light but Venus, the morning star. The officer, still bent on annihilating the enemies of his country, gave way to some profanity, and persisted in his order of shelling the rebels out of Venus.

When we left Union City we turned over our good A tents to our successors, and at Louisviile we were asked to take the shelter, or as the boys called them, dog tents, which were made of heavy muslin with buttons and holes to button two pieces together, each piece being as large as a sheet, and one to each man to carry. We rejected them and went down to Bridgeport without. We soon regretted our action, for while they were only a slender makeshift, they were better than nothing to shelter us, and we were unable to procure any until after the campaign was over, some time in December. We suffered very much for the use of them, and the best we could do was to improvise our ponchos, which were narrow for covering a tent, and it deprived us of the use of them when called to guard duty on a rainy day. In the meantime Gen. Rosencranz was relieved of the command and Gen. Grant became commander of the military division of the Mississippi. Soon we could see great activity on every hand, and we judged a move would soon be made toward the enemy. Gen. Hooker had brought the 11th and 12th army corps from the Potomac and we were attached to a brigade of the 11th corps, Gen. Howard commanding, Gen. Carl Schurz commanding the division, Col. Robinson, of the 82d Ohio, commanding the brigade. On the 27th of October a forward movement was made to open up communications more direct for supplies to reach the starving army at Chattanooga. Their horses and mules were nearly all dead from starvation, and the men could only procure a little parched corn for their subsistence. We started along the railroad that runs from Bridgeport to Chattanooga by Shellmound, Whitesides and Wauhatchie. We encountered no opposition till we came into Lookout Valley when the enemies pickets were driven in and some of them captured. The rebel batteries on Lookout Mountain opened upon us, but we were not to be deterred from our object and pressed on, occupying Brown's Ferry, about three miles from Chattanooga, securing the railroad and also the Tennesee river, which was navigable for light draft boats. We went into camp elated at our success. About midnight we were awakened by the roar of artillery and musket firing back at Wauhatchie, about three miles away, and soon we were on the march to lend a helping hand. The 12th corps was hotly engaged with Longstreet's corps, who had come down from Lookout Mountain to dislodge us before we were securely entrenched. But he found more than his match and, after sustaining a severe loss, he retreated back to the Mountain. We did not get fairly into the fight, but several volleys were fired into us as we moved up the valley, by the enemy that was posted on some foot hills at the base of Lookout. It tried our nerves very much to be fired on and not be permitted to return the compliment. For some reason we were ordered to hold our fire till we should receive orders. Several of us brought our guns to the shoulder to fire and were prevented by the Lieutenant, who said we must bide our time, and soon the enemy retired in great haste, and we laid on our arms till daylight. This action is known in history as the battle of Wauhatchie. Our regiment sustained no injury, the enemy over-shooting us, but several men had their guns struck on the barrel as they were carrying them at a right shoulder shift. The troops that bore the brunt of the battle, lost three or four hundred men in killed and wounded. The rebels lost more men and left their killed and some of their wounded for us to take care of. It was at this battle that a lot of our mules became stampeded and made toward the enemy's lines, who thought it was a cavalry charge and broke and fled in great haste, much to the amusement of our men when they found it out. We were no more assailed by the enemy's infantry while in Lookout valley. But they wrathfully used their artillery from the Mountain, and several were killed and wounded by their shells. Our regiment was in position behind a skirt of brushy timber that obscured their view of us, but if we made much fire they would try their artillery practice on us. The weather for some days was foggy and damp, and finally our Colonel got out of patience and said he would have a fire and dry his tent out, and if the rebels wanted to fire, they might fire away.

His servant built a fire of pine knots, that blazed up eight or ten feet high, making a splendid target for the foe, and soon the cannon on the point of Lookout belched forth its iron hail and threw the shell into the fire, but it buried itself in the soft ground and did not explode. The Colonel did not have time to call his servant, but proceeded to scatter the blazing faggots before another shot could be fired. The boys were amused at the haste with which the fire was extinguished, and when the cannon would crack as it frequently did, some one would hollow, look out Colonel, another shell's a coming, which he, of course, pretended not to hear. A man by the name of Petefish was sitting with his back to a tree, as a protection, when a shell came and struck the ground a few feet in front of him and exploded. A large piece flew back and struck him in the upper part of the chest, tearing it away and making a most ghastly wound, of which he soon died. Another man, Shoemaker by name, was sitting with his back to the enemy, over a small fire with his arms akimbo. A shot was fired and the shell took off his arm, and sank into the ground without exploding. We were subjected to this annoyance more than three weeks, and became inured to it, so that we seemed in a large measure indifferent, and held our ground 'till Grant was ready to dislodge them from Lookout Mountain and Missionary Ridge, which was successfully accomplished the 23d, 24th and 25th of November, 1863. Our picket line and the rebel's were close together, only Lookout Creek dividing us. By mutual agreement it was understood there was to be no picket-firing until one or the other party made an actual advance. This resulted in quite a correspondence between the belligerents on the picket line, and some trafficing occured, our men trading coffee for tobacco, which seemed quite beneficial to both parties. Sometimes taunts were thrown out in regard to who should finally whip, and the number of men each side could muster, etc., etc. I was greatly amused by hearing a colloquy between a Portuguese of our regiment and one of the rebels. Our man called out "say, Shonny Reb, how many men you got over dere?" The rebel replied 50,000, and 25,000 more coming. He evidently thought this was much more than we had, and he chuckled and asked, "Well, Yank, how many have you got?" "O, said DeSous, we'se got 100,000, and more dan 70,000 coming, and pretty soon, too." As Grant was heavily reinforced soon after by Sherman, and routed them from their strong positions, the Johnnie must have thought the little Portugese had the right figures. On Sunday, Nov. 22d, we left our camp in Lookout Valley, and marched into Chattanooga, and were halted near Fort Wood, and camped for the night. We found some other Illinois regiments and met with a number of old acquaintances, and Monday forenoon enjoyed quite a visit with them. None of us knew that in a few hours, we would be in a mortal combat, which would result in one of the greatest successes, to our arms, of the war. It was about two p. m., November 23d. The whole army as far as could be seen, were on parade, their guns brilliantly gleaming; it must have been an imposing sight, even to Bragg's Army, in their elevated position. Immediately the parade was changed into a charge, and we started for the enemy's position. Their picket line gave way and also their first line of works, which we held, capturing some prisoners, many men and horses on both sides being shot down, while there was fearful roaring of cannon and incessant rattle of smaller arms. Our forces seemed to rest and night came on, with some skirmishing till away after dark. We made our position stronger and then slept on our arms for the night. On the following morning the battle raged on the extreme right, where Hooker assailed Lookout Mountain, and fought his battle above the clouds. While there seemed to be comparative quiet in the center, where we lay ready to be called in to action any moment. Soon it was apparent that General Hooker had dislodged them from the Mountain and was turning the enemy's left, while Sherman was getting into position on our left, and securing a lodgment on the north end of Missionary

Ridge. It seems that Sherman's appearance in that locality was a surprise to the rebels, as they thought his forces were the troops massed in the center the afternoon of the 23d. In fact, while they were watching Thomas' and Hooker's troops, going into position on their left and center, Sherman disguised his movement behind the foothills, and the fog which prevailed obscured the view of the enemy on Lookout. He slipped across the Tennessee river near the mouth of South Chicamauga creek, and formed a lodgment on the north of Mission Ridge before the rebels were aware of it. It was related at the time, and generally believed by the soldiers of our command that under cover of darkness some of Sherman's men crossed the river and stealthily posting themselves between the rebel outside guard, and their reserve awaited the time of relieving the post. As the corporal's guard came near the Yankee he was halted in the usual form and told to advance and give the countersign, which he did, when the other men secreted, suddenly sprang up and took all the relief guard prisoners so quietly that no alarm was given, and then the cute Yankees proceeded to take off the remaining pickets, giving the countersign as requested and then taking them prisoners, till all were secured. Then going back to their reserve they took them in likewise.

This enabled Sherman to put down a pontoon bridge and get a division of men in position right across their flank before they knew anything about it. Whether this story is correct or not, one thing is certain that a sleek game was played by Sherman's men to so adroitly secure the position they did without being observed by the enemy. In the United States Colonial History there is a similar incident recorded, when Gen. Wolfe scaled the Heights of Abraham, and turned the French position, and compelled Montcalm to fight the battle of Quebec, in which both eminent commanders lost their lives.

On the 24th two incidents occurred which will be proper for me here to relate. We were lying in reserve, while Thomas' men were in action just beyond, but deadly missiles were flying all around. I don't know but what we were in nearly as much danger as the troops actually engaged. Indeed, such was the lay of the ground, that the enemy did a great deal of over-shooting, and, as Gen'l Grant, in his Memoirs, properly observes, "the Union soldier nearest the foe was in the least danger." We therefore, to escape the storm of lead, were ordered to lay flat on the ground, the bullets striking the trees all around us. In the meantime, two or three dogs started a rabbit, which bounded right for our ranks, the roar of battle and the yelping dogs frightening it almost out of its wits, and it was right among the prostrate soldiers before it knew of their presence. It ran right into the arms of a man named Charles Lazenby, and he caught it. Capt. Lightfoot, who evidently was watching the chase, as soon as he saw the rabbit taken in, jumped to his feet and offered a quarter for it. Lazenby, who was known to be a careful financier and always availed himself of an opportunity to turn an honest penny, accepted the offer, and cooly handed the rabbit over to the captain, who was equally self-possessed in the matter, and paid the money down. The ludicrousness of the thing, under the circumstances, provoked a good deal of merriment, tho' every man was hugging Mother Earth as close as possible to save his hide from being perforated by a rebel bullet. Shortly after this we heard tremendous cheering on the extreme right, in the direction of Lookout mountain, and all eyes were turned that way to discover the cause. It was a healthy Union cheer, so different from the screeching rebel yell that we were sure good fortune had come to Hooker's men. At this time the clouds so obscured the summit of the mountain, extending down perhaps half way to the base, and pretty soon they seemed to press down, as if preferring the valley for their fleeting movements, when suddenly the grand old stars and stripes appeared majestically waving above the clouds, the summit still obscured, but the clouds passing sufficiently low to reveal the flag and part of the rebel staff, from which it was now flying. Tens of thousands of men beheld the apparent phenomena of "Old Glory" planted in the very clouds, and knew what it augured for the Union cause, and again the glad refrain of loyal cheers reverberated through the valleys and re-echoed back from mountain slope. Our forces had carried Lookout mountain, crossed Chattanooga creek, and were driving the enemy back on the ill-fated battlefield of Chicamauga.

The night of the 24th it cleared up, and the 25th was bright, the sun shining clear overhead. We drew rations, and left the position we had held for nearly two days, Hooker's success making it unnecessary for so large a reserve force to be held there. The rebels appeared to be massing their forces against Sherman, who was seriously threatening their right. Howard's command was ordered to his support, so we started double-quick to where the battle was raging fiercely on our left. We passed many wounded men, and the ambulance, loaded with many more, hurrying to the Army of the Tennessee's field hospital, that was near the mouth of South Chicamauga creek. We met an ambulance that was conveying Gen'l Corse, who had been badly wounded in one of his limbs. He was regretting his misfortune very much, as I was told by Capt. Lightfoot, who heard him say: "Can't a man have an extra leg or two, so when he loses one he can take up another," mixing up his wandering talk with characteristic profanity. But we could only take a hurried glance at these things. On we sped, and soon Howard reported to Sherman. We went into position on the extreme left, swinging round nearly to the rear of Bragg's shattered forces. Finally we heard the troops in the center in heavy engagement, pressing the enemy. A tremendous cheer was heard, and it seemed as if the whole rebel force had gone up in smoke, or somewhere else; it disappeared from our front.

From Orchard Knob Grant had ordered a charge, to take the first of the rebel works, and then to wait for orders. Sheridan and Wood led the advance with their divisions. In a little while they were within the works. Flushed with victory and perhaps seized with an uncontrollable desire to avenge Chicamauga, they forgot orders, and hastened on and up, and penetrated the rebel lines near Bragg's headquarters, when they fled from every part of the field, Sherman's forces taking part in the pursuit, at Chicamauga Station. Guns, cannons, broken wagons, corn, meal and other provisions were scattered in profusion on the route, and the men scooped up the meal with their cups, as they ran, and put it in their haversacks, and passed on till the rebel hordes were driven out of Tennessee and speeding their way beyond Ringgold, Georgia.

On the afternoon of the 25th, or third day of the battle, while we were on the "double-quick" to reinforce Sherman, the sole of my shoe gave way, turned back, and tripped me up. I was considerably top-heavy, with three days' rations, a hundred rounds of cartridges, a blanket on my person, and gun at "right shoulder shift." The speed we were going it was impossible for me to recover, so I fell very hard, striking one of my knees on a small stump, bruising the cap severely and being very painful. However, I got up and went on with the command till we were halted for further orders. I think we perhaps rested half an hour or more. I was in great agony, and when I rose to my feet I found it impossible to proceed. I rolled up my pants and found my leg was greatly swollen and inflamed. The captain and orderly, seeing my condition, allowed me to drop out, and they went on and left me to my fate. As I lay there the battle continued to rage, but I was gratified to observe that it was moving farther away from me, indicating the victory for our forces. In spite of the din of battle and the hurrying past me of troops to the front, and the wounded to the rear and to the hospital, a feeling of lonesomeness came over me. No one paid me any attention and I could not help myself. Night was coming on and my comrades all far away, following up the retreating Confederates. Just at sundown an ambulance, with only two wounded men in it, approached. I hailed the driver, told him who I was and what was the matter with me. He said he only had orders to pick up the wounded of the 15th Corps and convey them to the hospital. I told him we had been detached from Thomas' army to reinforce Sherman; that I was far away from our own hospital and would have to remain there all night if I did not get help from him. At this he got out, and, with great difficulty, I was helped into the ambulance and conveyed to the field hospital of the 15th Corps. The surgeons were very busy, amputating limbs, extracting bullets from the wounded, and in other ways caring for them. The most needy cases of course received attention first. One of them came to me and examined my limb. Seeing I was helpless, but not dangerous, he remarked: "We'll attend to you after awhile." I never saw him again. For a week I was unable to walk, but did crawl down to the the river twice a day and bathed my bruised knee with cold water, which took out the inflammation and eased the pain, so that in a few days I could walk a little. My shoes were entirely worn out, and as I thought the men whose limbs were taken off would have no more use for shoes, I hobbled around to where the surgeons had performed their ghastly work, and there, among the mass of shoes, I found a pair. I do not think they belonged to the same man, but as they were right and left of the right size, I appropriated them, although they were spattered with the blood of their late owners. If it had not been for the exigencies of war, I should have considered it very shocking to have worn them. I got very tired of the hospital, and when I thought I could walk well enough to stand the trip, I went to Chattanooga and reported to the provost marshal there. He reported that the 11th Corps had gone with Sherman to reinforce Burnside at Knoxville and would likely be back before long, so he sent me to the soldiers' home to stay till they should return. I spent a couple of days there. A German soldier, of the 82d Illinois Regiment, was cooking what I took to be beef. As he seemed to have a good supply, I asked him if he could divide with me. We had had but a scant supply of pork for a long time, and I had had none of that since I was hurt. I had seen no beef for many weeks, and had been living on hard bread and coffee since leaving the regiment. The cooking beef was making my mouth water. The boy told me to help myself. I cooked and ate the meat with agreeable relish, and then asked my German friend where he had procured so much beef. A broad grin spread over his countenance as he replied: "Yaw, it vas a beese of moole." I was a little taken back, but I had eaten it with such keen relish that I was not sentimental enough to "heave up Jonah," though I was sure the mule meat was taken from one of those unfortunate animals that had perished by starvation and been dead perhaps many days.

CHAPTER VI.

One afternoon the provost marshal came over to the soldiers' home with two citizens who claimed to be, and I think were, loyal men. They wanted some security from the visits of marauding soldiers. They concluded to send me and another man to be quartered in their homes as safeguards till we were relieved. They were to board and lodge us while we remained with them. The gentleman that I went with was a David Hammel, an old resident, and a justice of the peace. His family consisted of a wife, two sons and one daughter, under age, and a married daughter, whose husband had been forced into the rebel army, but he had deserted, and was then in our naval service, on the gunboat Princeton. They had some wheat flour, meal and bacon, that somehow had escaped the foragers of both armies, and a good bed was given me. As that was the coldest winter ever known in the country, it was an acceptable arrangement for me, as I continued quite lame. I found a musket one day that the rebels had thrown away in their precipitate retreat from Lookout Mountain. It was the same kind we carried, but the barrel was bent into a triangle shape. The lock on my gun was defective and did not always explode the cap, so it occurred to me I could change the lock and perhaps secure a better one. It did not occur to me that the bent gun might be loaded, as there was no cap on. I put one on to test it, holding it carelessly in front of me, and pulled the trigger, when it went off, with a tremendous bang, knocking me down. The charge came out at the curve, which was perhaps cracked a little by the bending. I soon recovered, and was not much worse for the shock. I should have been surprised if the charge had followed the crooked barrel, made a circle, and shot me in the back.

I stayed with the family about four weeks. It seems the provost marshal had forgotten us. I was so afraid of being regarded as a deserter that I wrote to Capt. Lightfoot, telling him about my condition and where I was. The regiment, as I afterwards learned, was at Kelly's Ferry, about eight miles from Chattanooga, in good winter quarters. He went to Chattanooga and inquired of the provost marshal about me, but he seemed to have forgotten all about me. As provisions were running pretty short, I told Mr. Hammel I thought I ought to try and find my regiment. I thought matters were now settled so that I was not needed, and also that they had need of the provisions yet remaining. He said he thought perhaps I was right, but said I had been so long as one of the family they were all loth to see me go away. So one morning I bid them "good-bye," and went down to Chattanooga, where I reported to the same officer. When he saw me he knew me well enough, and knew Mr. Hammel, too. He informed me of the whereabouts of my regiment, but did not say a word about Capt. Lightfoot's visit to him, so there has always been a doubt in my mind about the captain seeing the right officer. I then took up my line of march to Kelly's Ferry, crossing over the ground of Hooker's famous battle, which has become historic, and, as a war incident, known to every household in the land. It was three miles from Hammel's to Chattanooga and eight from there to Kelly's, and I was very lame and tired when I reached the regiment. When the officers heard my story and saw my condition, they said I was foolish for coming. I might have stayed all winter in those comfortable quarters. I thought, however, I had done right to report for duty again. The army supplies were now abundant; the men had drawn new clothing, looked well, and evidently were having a good time for soldiers in time of war. About two weeks after I returned the regiment was ordered back to Bridgeport, Ala. We relieved a Kentucky regiment, who had built good winter quarters, expecting to stay. It vexed them to think they had to leave them, and a rumor got out that a colored regiment was to take their place. They became furious, and pulled down and set fire to their quarters. We arrived before they left, and when they saw we were a respectable veteran regiment, and about as white as they were; also that we had left comfortable quarters in repair for some one else, they seemed sorry at their vandalism. This cool, or warm, reception, as it may be construed either way, did not disconcert us. We went to work, and in two or three days were as comfortably fixed as we had been at Kelly's. During this time both armies, in the main, were quiet. Patrol parties were frequently sent out to scour the country and pick up rebel soldiers, that were deserters or furloughed from their command. Our scouts generally knew all that happened, and when rebels were anywhere near our lines we soon found it out, and a squad would be sent to try and bring them in. I was out on several excursions of this kind. A detail would be made from the several companies and regiments of the brigade, and, under the command of a captain or lieutenant, would leave camp just after dark and roam over the country for captures of this kind.

We were out one night on this business, and

were pretty sure of our game, as a scout had reported certainly the return of a man to visit his family, and led us to the house where his people lived. We found his father and mother, very old people, his wife and two small children, but they declared that Jim had not been at home for nearly two years. A guard was stationed round the house, and the lieutenant went in, with four men, to search the house, but did not find him. I was posted near a tobacco house, and I heard some noise in the upper part of it. Two of us went in carefully, but it was so dark we could see nothing. We groped round awhile, and then we thought we would see if we could reach anything above. We pointed our bayonets up, and found some loose boards laid on the joists. When we moved them, dirt and trash fell down and nearly suffocated us. Finally we struck a board that was more solid, but which sprung a little, like some weighty object was upon it. We concluded it was a man, and, in very strong language, we commanded him to come down. He could hear our guns click as we cocked them, and, fearing we would shoot, he told us he would come down and give himself up. When we got outside, he begged that he might be taken in to see his folks before we marched him away. The lieutenant came out about this time, and we asked him about it. He was a man of kind heart, and said: "Of course, take him in, but be careful, don't stay too long; let him kiss his wife and babies and come out, for we will be late getting back to camp." His parents and wife looked very foolish when they saw two Yankees bringing Jim in, but soon realized the situation, and broke down entirely, weeping and moaning piteously. We were touched by this affecting scene, and tried to console them by saying we would not hurt him if he did not try to get away. After he had affectionately kissed them all, we took him away. He told me he had just got home that day, having been away two years, and it was the most trying experience of his life. By way of consolation, I told him it might be the best thing that ever happened to him. If he did not try to escape, he would likely be sent to Camp Chase, where he would be comfortably quartered and fed, and perhaps never see active service again, till the war was over, when he could return home. What effect these words had upon him I do not know. With a number of others, he was sent north, and that was the last we ever saw of him.

On another occasion we were out, and, approaching a little bunch of houses, called Hamburg, we were startled by seeing something like tents. The captain called a halt, and a kind of council of war was held to consider what we should do. There were about twenty men in the squad, and of course we could not think of attacking a force as large as the supposed tents would indicate. None of the men had ever been there before, except myself and a man from Company C. by the name of Moore. In talking the matter, all felt sure that what we saw were tents, except Moore and I. The captain was most positive, and said if we were of sufficient force we might charge them and take them in, but, as it was, he thought we had better slip quietly away and not disturb them. I then spoke up and said I had been there twice before; that there was a big spring close by, and the women came from some distance round about and did their washing there; that I thought it was clothes hung out to dry which were mistaken for tents. Moore also spoke and confirmed what I said. The captain then said: "Are you two men willing to leave us here and crawl up as close as you can and see whether they are tents or not?" I said I was perfectly willing to go and Moore also assented, so we struck out. We proceeded cautiously for awhile, when I said: "Moore, a company of rebels would be fools to come and pitch tents and go into camp so near to as large an army as ours; I am confident it's nothing but a few clothes hung on the bushes." He just laughed out loud, so the boys must have heard him. As we approached nearer we soon saw we were not mistaken, and Moore said: "Let us charge, and take the town ourselves, and then make a little fun of captain and the boys." "All right," said I, and we sent up a cheer that made the welkin ring and started double-quick for the works of the enemy. I don't suppose two men ever made so much noise. Two hungry dogs came out to dispute our way, but, catching a glimpse of our shining bayonets, they broke for taller timber, and left us complete masters of the situation. We found a few old women, that were considerably scared at the noise we made, but, as we didn't molest them, they soon quieted down, and great peace prevailed in the city of Hamburg. The captain and his men came marching in, and, in view of his superior rank, we turned the city over to him. He interrogated the women with a few questions, but, getting nothing out of them but monosyllables, he became disgusted, and gave the command to return to camp, which we reached just as day was breaking.

These were some of the experinces we had, otherwise it was a quiet winter, and we seemed nearly as far removed from hostilities as if we were north of the Ohio. The paymaster made us a visit, which was very acceptable, as we had not seen him for some time and there was over six months pay due us. We also turned in our Springfield muskets and drew the Enfield, which was a superior gun—would shoot stronger and more accurately than any we ever had. This was the fourth variety of firearm we had used, and I believe it was the best. We used it in actual conflict more than any other gun, so I suppose the number of victims was greater.

There was an extraordinary fall of snow on the 22d of March, from fifteen to twenty inches deep. Peach trees were in full bloom, and it was a novel sight to see them in the midst of snow. The oldest inhabitant said he had never seen the like in that country before, and that they would have to give up the conflict if the Yankees were going to bring down the northern climate with them, as well as their armies, for it was enough to endure to stand the charges of our soldiers, let alone the blasts of a northern winter. For two or three days it was severe on the men who did guard duty, but it soon melted, and the weather became very fine. By May 1, 1864, Gen. W. T. Sherman, who had been appointed to the command of the "Military Division of the Mississippi," had everything in readiness to move, and we retraced our steps to Chattanooga. The 11th and 12th Corps were consolidated and called the 20th Corps of the "Army of the Cumberland." Gen. Joseph Hooker commanded the corps and Gen. G. H. Thomas the army. The "Army of the Tennessee" was commanded by Gen. J. B. McPherson, and the "Army of the Ohio" by Gen. J. M. Schofield. Several changes occurred in our regimental officers. Cols. Fox, Wyatt and Newman, the last two being Lieutenant-Colonels, had resigned and gone home. Capt. Lightfoot and Lieut. Shafer, of our company, had also resigned. J. B. LaSage, who commanded Co. A, became Lieut.-Col. and commanded the regiment; N. B. Brown, Captain of Co. B, became Major; B. F. Hilligoss became Captain of Co. G, and Theop Ayers, First Lieutenant. I think all these officers remained with the regiment until the war was over. The organization of the army for the spring campaign was perfect. Nearly all the regiments were veterans, who were thoroughly equipped, and possessed of a good deal of confidence in their officers and themselves, which made them well nigh invincible. It is doubtful if a more efficient army was ever marshalled than the one Sherman led from Chattanooga to Atlanta and from there to the sea; then to Raleigh, N. C., when the collapse of the rebellion came. It was an imposing sight to see the "men in blue" and their arms glistening in the sun, the colors pointing south. A little distance off the marching column looked like a huge serpent winding itself through the valleys and across the mountains. Then there was the artillery, with their two hundred and fifty cannon and three thousand horses to draw them. There was also seven thousand cavalry, and whole number of men—about one hundred thousand—with a vast train of wagons, each wagon usually drawn by six mules, and several thousand of them, making a wonderful equipment for aggressive warfare.

CHAPTER VII.

We soon came in contact with the rebel forces, which were now commanded by Gen. Joseph E. Johnston, who was perhaps the equal of Gen. R. E. Lee in military ability. His army occupied a strongly entrenched position at Dalton, Georgia. The names of places occupied by the rebels give some indication of the natural strength of them: Rockyfaced Ridge and Buzzard Roost. These were made doubly strong by fortifying. I suppose if Gen. Sherman had undertaken to carry this position by assault he might have lost half his army and then not succeeded. He merely threatened it with Thomas' army, while McPherson slipped into Snake Creek Gap and so threatened the rear of Johnston's army that he was compelled to retreat on Resacca. At this point the enemy was assailed on the 15th of May. Hooker's corps fought quite a battle, and our regiment got in some very bloody work. They succeeded in completely investing the enemy's works, capturing a battery. The whole rebel army gave way, and that night got across the Oustenaula river. The entire loss of the army was six hundred killed and thirty-five hundred wounded.

Our regiment lost thirty-five men killed and wounded. It sustained a good fighting reputation. Gen. Hooker observed them going into position under a heavy fire. The movement, deliberately performed as if on parade, called from that officer a handsome compliment. It was impossible to bring Johnston's army to anything like a stand for some distance. The retreat was conducted with the consummate skill characteristic of the general who led them. The southern papers, in explaining the situation, said the Fabian policy was being enacted. That Johnston was simply decoying Sherman from his base, and, at the opportune moment, he would entangle him in such inextricable difficulties, then turn upon him and crush him to irrecoverable atoms. A brilliant conception that was never realized. Some skirmishing took place with the rear guard, but the finest portion of northern Georgia was relinquished, almost without a struggle, and Rome, Kingston, Adairsville, Cassville and some other towns were occupied; we passed on to the Etawah river, to find the bridges burned and the enemy a way beyond. The pontoons were brought into requisition, and good bridges put down, so that the delay was only trifling. A pontoon bridge is made of flat-bottomed boats, stationed several feet apart, and held stationary in the stream by anchors; stringers are put from boat to boat, joined fast together; then plank is laid across the stringers, and it forms a good bridge The boats, of course, give some beneath the weight that passes over them, but a marching column of men, observing "the route step," can about as safely cross a rapid stream as if it were a solid structure, built of wood or stone. The heavy artillery, with the six mule teams, and heavy loaded wagons, got across safely. In fact, I do not remember a single accident that befell us in all that extraordinary campaign. These boats were first made entirely of wood, but in order to economize in weight and bulk, the pontoons with Sherman's army were just wooden frames, covered with thick, heavy canvas, and made entirely water-proof. This facilitated matters very much saved a great deal in the way of transportation and rendered the crossing of a stream a comparatively insignificant matter to the go-ahead Yankees

Our advance resulted in the capture of many prisoners, some of them being taken in actual conflict, while a great many, taking advantage of the retreat, slipped out of the ranks, and, hiding themselves from their officers till their army had passed on and ours had advanced, they came out of their hiding and gave themselves up. These perhaps, were mainly conscripts, and some, being impressed with the invincible manner in which the campaign was being conducted on our part, lost heart in their cause, and voluntarily became prisoners, as the shortest and most certain way to finish their part of the great tragedy that was being enacted. These wholesale desertions were frequent during the Atlanta campaign. The disaffected, who had done nothing to bring the war on and had really no personal interest in the success of the Confederates, had found out that the Union prisons were not obnoxious in severity and short supplies; in fact, if a Confederate, tired of the war, wanted his liberty, he could usually secure it by taking the oath, which many did, thus escaping the military service of the South, and saved their lives. Some of them even enlisted in our army and navy, and stayed till the war was ended.

An incident occurred just before our army crossed the Chattahoochie river. One afternoon our men had halted to camp, and, as was usual on breaking ranks, the men would scatter somewhat to procure wood and stakes to fix their tents, and frequently to pick blackberries, which were then ripe and abounded everywhere in that country. One of the boys had strayed a considerable distance from his comrades, lured away by the tempting fruit. He was about to retrace his steps when he heard a slight noise; as if some person near had stepped on a stick and broken it. He looked up, and behold! right close were five Confederates, coming towards him. Being without arms and defenseless, he thought he was a prisoner. His excitement prevented him from seeing they were also unarmed. He said he could not run; his heart seemed to mount up nearly to his throat, and he became, as it were, transfixed. The Johnnies were the first to speak, and, evidently comprehending his embarrassment, said they did not want to take him but they wanted to be taken, which, to him, "was as good news from a far country." He then saw they were without arms, and the truth flashed upon him. With their voluntary consent, he became their escort to headquarters, where they were reported and afterwards sent north.

After crossing the Etawah river, we found the enemy in a very strong position at Pumpkin Vine creek, and Hooker's corps, and particularly the first division, were led into an ambuscade, sustaining a terrific fire from batteries and musketry, yet they held their ground, and bivouaced for the night, taking care of their wounded and burying their dead. This was the severest loss sustained by our regiment in action: about eighty killed and wounded. Our color bearer, Aleck Crouse, was shot dead. He was a man of fine appearance, upwards of six feet in height, well proportioned and straight as an arrow—a brave soldier and genial companion under all circumstances. Great care was taken to mark his grave, and shortly after the war was over his relatives conveyed him to Illinois and buried him with his kindred.

The Confederates were not easily dislodged from this formidable position, and for a number of days they held us at bay. Once they massed their forces and charged our position. We were now able to avenge the great loss sustained on the 25th. Our men reserved their fire till they were very close, when batteries and small arms belched forth their storm of iron and lead, and they were repulsed with fearful loss. We finally compelled them to seek another well fortified position, on Kenesaw mountain. Thus it was, when driven or flanked out of their strongholds, they had another to go into just as strong, disputing every inch of our progress, so that for days and weeks it was a continuous battle or skirmish. We may safely affirm that for a period of four months during the progress of this campaign there was scarcely a day but what some part of the army was engaged in either a skirmish or a battle, so that the report of firearms was almost incessantly heard. This made picket duty very arduous, as well as dangerous, for men on post had to fortify, to screen themselves from the enemy's pickets and sharpshooters. When an officer or private was detailed for picket duty it seemed like a special opportunity to lay down his life for the country. Very many brave men, in this way, served their last detail, and never returned to tell the story of their valor. It was a time to test real courage and soldierly prowess. Many perhaps shrank from the ordeal, but their soldierly pride impelled them to control their feelings and meet the dire responsibility that was upon them. A few cases only of actual cowardice occurred that I know of. A captain was detailed for picket duty; he had not been at his post long when he feigned illness and was allowed to retire. A lieutenant was next on detail, and, like a true man that he was, he unflinchingly took his post. Sometime during the day he became a target for a sharpshooter, and was killed in the line of duty. His lifeless form was brought inside the works, his company uttering a wail of anguish and threats of vengeance, for he was greatly beloved by his men, and they felt he was a victim to the cowardice of the captain he had relieved. Whether the men were just in their conclusions or not, it became very unpleasant for the captain. One day, when all was comparatively quiet, the solitary report of a musket was heard, and a stray bullet went through the captain's tent, striking uncomfortably close to his person. This aroused his suspicions, and not long after he resigned for the good of the service. This was the same officer who, a few months before, when in command of a patrol squad, wanted to hie away from a few clothes on bushes, his heated imagination picturing a vast number of tents filled with hundreds of rebels.

One strange feature in the case of men wounded was that some recovered from very serious wounds, while others, slightly injured, as we thought, would die of their wounds. On the 25th of May, I think it was, a private named W. D. Lindsay was supposed to be mortally wounded, as he received a minie ball in the breast, going through the back, but he recovered sufficiently to be transferred to the Invalid corps, where he served till the close of the war, and was living twenty years afterwards. Edward Hickman had a slight wound in the arm, but for some cause he could not rally, and after a long period of suffering he died. He was a man past the military age, being over forty-five, and was a very devoted Christian. In earlier life he had been a drunkard, but he became a Christian some years before the war, and lived what he professed, commanding the respect of all the men. He was so exact in his morals he thought it wrong to forage provisions from the enemy, and, when this was a necessity, some one else always supplied his needs, as he would have starved before he would have done it. He seemed, however, very conscientious that shooting at the enemies of his country in time of action was all right, and would draw a bead on a rebel as cooly as he would to shoot a vicious animal. He informed me that at the affair at Holly Springs he took deliberate aim at a mounted rebel, and it was a matter of great satisfaction to him that he saw the rebel drop from the saddle. Whether a man, in his country's service, is more justified in taking life than property is an ethical question I could not solve as he did, for, under a pressure of military necessity, I would rather be guilty of foraging than the death of any poor mortal. At a pleasant wrangle over the rightfulness of foraging, a man by the name of Cruse twitted Hickman a little. "Why," said he, "Mr. Hickman, I can prove it is right to steal sometimes." "No, James, you cannot." "Yes," insisted Cruse, "I can even prove it to you it's right to steal sometimes." Hickman became enthusiastic in favor of the eighth commandment, and when all became amused at his intense interest for right and rectitude, his tormentor explained his position by saying, "It's right to steal away from bad company," when Hickman exclaimed, "Oh! James, you are a naughty boy!"

W. A. Young was wounded badly in the arm, the ball tearing out the muscular part between the elbow and shoulder. It was bad for a long time, but he recovered so as to admit of service in the Invalid corps, where he completed his term of service. A recruit named Spencer was slightly wounded, close to Young. He set up a piteous cry, and said if he was home with his mother he would never go to war again. This man was very brave when he first came to the regiment. He said he wanted to kill half-a-dozen rebels the first fight he got into. This little scratch quite unmanned him, and he was glad to retire without reaching the goal of his ambition. He was sent to the hospital, and somehow got a discharge, and was never seen in mortal combat again.

About July 1st Johnston was compelled to cross the Chattahoochie river, where we enjoyed a brief respite from active hostilities, and, being about eight miles from Atlanta, we could see the city. The enemy's position across the river was very strongly fortified, but Uncle Billy, as the soldiers familiarly called Sherman, arranged to get them out by the usual flank movement, and crossed the river above their fortifications, proceeding, without opposition, in the direction of

Atlanta. About this time I had a conversation with W. C. Young, of our company. He was considerably older than myself, and had seen more of the world—had been across the plains and in California, and had become inured to danger before the war. I was not a professing Christian at this time, but in belief was radically orthodox, while my friend was a pronounced skeptic. We sometimes discussed these points of difference between us. Once he made the assertion that the Bible was a bundle of absurdities and contradictions and not worthy the endorsement of sensible men. I asked him to prove it. "Well," he remarked, "there is the ridiculous story of Samson catching a thousand foxes, tying fire-brands to their tails, and turning them loose in the cornfields of the Philistines, burning them down. Now," he says, "I'd like to have you tell me how he held them till he tied them." This raised a loud laugh, and the boys thought I was worsted so bad I could not reply. When their mirth had subsided, I said: "Well, Young, that can be explained from a common sense standpoint, and does not of necessity involve a miracle, although it might have been one. You know Samson was noted for being a leader in Israel, as well as for his great physical strength. As such, like a general in these times, he could devise a plan of operations and then execute them by aid of his army of assistants. We say Gen. Grant took Ft. Donalson. We mean he took it with his army of forty thousand men. So Samson, as the head of the nation, the judge of Israel, is said to do such and such things. Then, in the brief recital of Bible history, we have few details; the substance of the fact is all that is aimed at. We may not be confined to this explanation; we may concede that he did it single-handed and alone and not involve an absurdity or a contradiction. It does not say he caught them all at once; he may have caught them on several different occasions and turned out a few braces at a time or as many as he could handle conveniently. Then," I remarked, "the fun would have lasted longer; like our present unpleasantness, it would be more than a "breakfast spell," and the strong man would have enjoyed it hugely. Then matters are simplified greatly, from the fact that it was not a thousand foxes, but only three hundred." I had now the laugh on him. He made no other explanation, and the boys were much amused that he was discomfitted in the argument, for they were generally orthodox in belief if not very good practical Christians.

But to return to our conversation. Young was that morning feeling very blue. The heavy losses we had sustained was weighing heavily on his mind, and he had a presentiment that in the next battle he would not come out alive. I said, "O, Bill, you must not give way to your feelings now; you have braved so many dangers that you might believe you will providentially escape till the war is over, and then you can see your Tilly again," that was the name of a young woman he had married when he was at home, a paroled prisoner, and with whom he was deeply in love. The tears trickled down his cheeks at the mention of her name, and he said he would never see her again. I vainly endeavored to console him, but he insisted that he would be slain in the next battle. About this time the Confederate author'ties, becoming dissatisfied with the Fabian policy of Joe Johnston, relieved him of the command and Gen. Hood was appointed to succeed him. There was a change in the Confederate tactics. Instead of retreating from one position to another, Hood resolved to strike the flanks of Sherman while in motion and not protected by breastworks, a plan if adopted earlier in the campaign might have resulted in some temporary advantage to them, but nothing could have successfully resisted Sherman's advance with the relative strength of the contending armies being as it was, and whatever dispositions the enemy made, they must finally have yielded to the superior numbers of the Union army. Accordingly on the 20th of July, as Thomas was moving in the direction of Atlanta, and had just crossed Peach Tree creek, Hooker's corps had halted for a short sason, their arms stacked in line of battle. The enemy came on them in the fearful onset of a charge. It was so sudden that our men had barely time to take their guns and commence shooting at the advancing foe. At some points the combatants came right together so as to club their muskets and snatch the colors from each other. I was told by the members of the 136th New York regiment that their colors were thus snatched away from them three times, and as many times recovered in the same desperate way, when the enemy spent the force of their charge and retired. It seems that the rebels had not calculated very accurately the distance they would have to come, and we were farther off than they had expected, so they were considerably exhausted by their run, and our men being the freshest, gave them the advantage. It has been said that the southern man was fiercer and for a short time more effective, but his reserve force was sooner spent than his Yankee antagonist. It seems that Grant calculated something on this, for he observes after a sanguinary conflict, in which both were largely exhausted, the first that assaulted was sure to win. He was careful to first resume the offensive, and usually won the battle. Our men in this bloody battle certainly outwinded the Confederates, and they sullenly retired within their entrenchments. Our loss was very great; our regiment left nearly forty on the field in killed and wounded, my friend Young being among the mortally wounded. As soon as I could I visited the field hospital where our wounded lay thick, with every conceivable wound that could be inflicted upon a mortal frame. Young had a frightful wound in the abdomen, and he knew he could not live. He was, however, perfectly conscious and called my attention to our conversation the day before. Of course, I remembered it well enough, yet tried to console him by saying that his feelings, if he could be hopeful, would have much to do with his recovery. He shook his head mournfully, and said he knew the nature of the wound, and it was utterly impossible for him to get well. "O," said he, "John, I don't want to die yet! O, it is so dark before me; everything is so dark! so dark!" I could not repress my feelings, and I knew I could give no consolation, so turning away, so he would not be affected by my emotion, I wept at the thought of the untimely death of my skeptical friend. He was moved back to the hospital at Marietta, and soon died; his grave may now be found at the National cemetery there. I met his bereaved companion soon after my return from the war. She was dressed in deep mourning, and when she saw me at the reception given our regiment, she came and congratulated me on my return, and said she was glad to see so many of the boys return. "But, O! its too bad, too bad, that Will had to be left down there", and broke down entirely in a paroxysm of grief. It is said she gave way to despondency from which her friends tried to rally her. After a few years her burdened heart could endure no more, and she sickened and died, no doubt the victim of a broken heart.

The army now pressed closely to the enemy's fortified position. McPherson, on the left received a similar attack which was well nigh successful, this noble Union general being slain. Gen. Logan, however, took the command and by his extraordinary valor, the battle was gained for the Union arms. The same tactics were tried again on July 28, but Sherman had so arranged his forces as to ward off the blow much easier. This seems to have satisfied Hood that he could not defeat the Union army by these methods, and he seemed content to remain inside his works, assuming the strictly defensive policy. Large as our army was, we could not entirely invest the extensive works of Atlanta. Their communications on the south remained open, but we pressed them so that they were almost entirely besieged. Our guns were turned upon the city, making it very uncomfortable for the citizens; some of their suburban residences were outside their fortifications; these were riddled, and some of them destroyed by our artillery. One of them known as the Potter house was used by them as a cover for their sharpshooters, and though many shot and shell were thrown into it, they continued to harrass our line by their accurate firing from it. Such was their range of our position that if a person showed his head above the parapet, it would call for a shot from this house. One day an officer belonging to the battery we were supporting had been sleeping in his tent, and on awakening he seems to have forgot the precaution to keep his head low, when he was fired on, the ball entering the center of his forehead; he fell dead near where I was sitting. One day I had occasion to go for water to a spring between the works and the picket line. I was careful when climbing over the works to not expose my person more than was necessary, but getting farther down the slope, I thought I was out of sight, if not out of reach, and began to walk upright, carelessly swinging my canteens as I went along. Suddenly five shots were fired striking the front and rear of me and making the dirt fly over me; I then stooped over again and ran down to the springs, filled my canteens and started back, retaining the stooped-over position till I was safely inside the works. This was such an annoyance that it was determined to break it up, so a picked detail of men crept up as close as possible, unobserved by the sharpshooters. It was a large two story building right under their guns, and they were in the upper story for better observation and execution, and were looking away beyond the stealthy Yankees crawling upon them, and were greatly surprised when our men broke in upon their safe retreat and demanded their surrender. As they saw it was useless to resist, they were speedily disarmed, the buildings fired and the whole squad, with the prisoners, hurried to our lines before the artillery could be trained on them or a force sent out to intercept them. This effectually broke up that nest and we were not bothered by them again. We continued to invest Atlanta without gaining a decided advantage. Hood kept close within his works; a continual artillery duel was maintained, failing to intimidate or seriously injure us. The buildings of the city did not fare so well under our fire; many were riddled and in some instances they took fire and burned down. The skirmishing on the picket was continuous, but did not result in any great advantage to either party.

CHAPTER VIII.

This did not exactly suit our restive commander, and he arranged for raising the siege and using the main part of the army against the enemy's communications. The 20th Corps, under Slocum (as Gen. Hooker left the army soon after the death of McPherson), was ordered back to protect the bridge across the Chattahoochie, occupying a strongly entrenched position, so that he would be able to defend successfully against the whole rebel army till he could be reinforced by Sherman. In the meantime, the main army moved round the right of Atlanta and struck the West Point railroad at East Point, thoroughly destroying it. Gen. Howard went into position at Jonesboro, and met the enemy in a severe engagement, being reinforced by Thomas. They drove them in great confusion from the field. This was a hand to hand encounter for awhile, the rebels stubbornly resisting our advance as long as possible, when the superior endurance of the Yankees prevailed and the Confederates fled from the field, Hardee's forces barely escaping capture. An incident of this battle was related to me, indicating the proximity of the belligerents. A powerful German, a lieutenant of the 14th Ohio, whose name was Frank Fleck, threw down his sword, and went at them with his fists, knocking down a half dozen or more, and, catching a brigade commander, he pulled him over the works, by main strength and awkwardness, exclaiming: "Mein Gott, I've no batience mit you." I saw this incident related in McElroy's Prison Life several years after the war, and when I was pastor of the M. E. Church at Richland, Iowa, in 1886, I met Fleck there, a member of the G. A. R. Post, and engaged in the butcher business. I asked him about the story, and he said it was substantially correct.

When our army left the entrenched position before Atlanta the enemy thought it was a retreat and that Sherman had given up the attempt to capture the city. There was great rejoicing thereat, and it was reported that the people of Macon came up to congratulate them on their good fortune. What must have been their consternation when, a few days afterwards, the invincible Sherman, with his army, was destroying the railroad and communications twenty or thirty miles south of Atlanta. They had neither time nor inclination to assail Slocum's position at the Chattahoochie, if they had ever thought of it. They had now to evacuate Atlanta and mass their forces against Sherman, as their only alternative.

Early on the morning of September 2d great explosions were heard in the direction of Atlanta, and Gen. Slocum, rightly divining that Hood was blowing up his munitions, put his command in motion towards the city. Our brigade was in the lead and our regiment in advance. When we came to our old works there was no opposition incurred; we therefore pressed forward, and were soon at the enemy's strong fortifications, covering the city. These, likewise, were deserted, and, with triumphant cheers, we entered the city, and soon raised "Old Glory," the National emblem, over the Franklin printing office, where we found a staff that, a few hours before, had floated the Confederate rag. The 101st Illinois always claimed they were the first troops to enter Atlanta. Some others have claimed the honor, and it is possible that, owing to the size of the place and the number of men marching on it, different commands may have gone into the city nearly simultaneously. The honor, however, is an empty one, for to enter a city whose defenders have fled from it is not worth contending for. We should concede that the co-operative efforts of all the forces in and around Atlanta had made its capture possible. The twaddle about who went in first puts me in mind of the enraptured artist at Niagara Falls, contemplating the sublime downpour of the cataract, exclaiming: "How wonderfully the water comes down!" when a crude Irishman remarked: "Be jabers, and what's to hinder it?" What could hinder any Yankee force from taking a stronghold whose defenders had all fled?

Our regiment was retained as special guards and to operate the fire department of the city, being exempt from regular picket duty and allowed the freedom of the city. In a few days Sherman's forces came in from Jonesboro, and all were camped in and around the late rebel stronghold. enjoying a brief respite from the arduous and bloody conflicts in which they had been engaged. By the capture of Atlanta the Confederacy sustained an irreparable loss. If the capture of Vicksburg was cutting the Confederacy in two, this was cutting it into quarters, and depriving the foe of a large tract of country which contributed largely of the supplies to their armies. If, in all reason, they should have laid down their arms when their defeat at Gettysburg demonstrated that they could never successfully invade the North, certainly when they could not hold the Gate City of the South, so far in the interior, they should have yielded the contest, and saved many valuable lives and much property. But Jefferson Davis was something of a historian, and he seems to have thought that the fratricidal war in America had European precedent. And, as the Russians had annihilated Bonaparte, in the heart of their country, in 1812, Sherman's hordes, likewise, might be disposed of in the same way. He therefore went through the South, making speeches in several cities, citing these things, to encourage his people in the forlorn hope of yet driving Sherman back. This was letting the "cat out of the bag," and Gen. Sherman says he was not slow to profit by the information these speeches imparted. The first indication of Davis' project being carried out was Hood's attack on our communications. He struck the railroad at several points and captured a few small garrisons. Sherman, for awhile, disposed his forces to checkmate him, and a desultory campaign was carried on, in which Altoona Pass was the severest battle fought. A large force, under Gen. French, attacked Gen. Corse's command furiously, but were repulsed with great loss, and, Sherman sending a good reinforcement, the rebel commander was compelled to relinquish his object and beat a hasty retreat. Here Sherman signaled from Kenesaw Mountain to Gen. Corse to "Hold the Fort, for I am Coming." This laconic reply has become a household word, and indeed, the basal thought of a favorite religious song. The object of Hood was evidently to decoy Sherman out of Georgia, and further, if he could, when the latter devised a plan of operations to allow Hood to go North and he would go South. Thereupon he divided the army, leaving the 4th, 16th and 23d Corps, with other detachments, to Gen. Thomas. He retained the 14th, 15th, 17th and 20th Corps for the great march to the sea. The wisdom of this disposition of forces was demonstrated, by Thomas completely destroying Hood's army at Nashville, December 15th and 16th, and the triumphant march to the sea. During Hood's raid the 20th Corps remained at Atlanta, and it was a time of rest and recuperation to them. The most exciting thing was the presidential election, but it was so one-sided as to lose much of the interest that is usually manifested on such occasions, the men mainly voting for Lincoln. The State of Illinois had made no provision for the soldiers to vote in the field, but the government ordered the vote, and it was carefully and honestly taken, for some purpose, which I never knew. The state, however, went strongly Republican, and the soldier vote was not needed. Most of the other states had their soldier vote legally taken, and it was counted in the general result of those states.

For about two weeks before we left Atlanta we began to get ready for our march, though none of us knew where we were going. A general destruction of everything that could be of service to our enemies was ordered. It was truly painful to see the wanton waste of property, but no doubt the terrible exigency of war demanded it. The inhabitants had been compelled to leave, by Sherman's orders, for he did not want to furnish provisions for them, and their own necessities would have compelled their exile in the event of the government not providing for them. In the summer of 1895, being in Atlanta, I casually observed to an old resident that I had been one of the men who had assisted in pulling their town to pieces and burning it up, and had not been back since. "Oh," said he, "that was the best thing that ever happened us. Of course I didn't see it that way then, and was all-fired mad about it at the time. Why, we've built a good deal better town, and if Sherman had not destroyed it as he did it's likely the old dingy buildings would have been standing yet. Now we've got everything new, and many thousand more people than we had then, and I doubt if there is another city that can show such prosperity in all the land." I was glad he was not inclined to regard me as a vandal for my part in the matter, and we enjoyed a pleasant conversation about it. The negro auction blocks were a matter of interest to me, with their large, lettered signs: "Negroes bought and sold here." These were all obliterated, and have never been seen since. The wrath of an invading army is always inveterately exercised against railroad property that they do not expect to use, so, when we were going to leave Atlanta, everything of this kind was utterly destroyed. The whole system of Southern railways must have been well-nigh ruined by the vandalism of both armies, but, as you travel in the South to-day, railway enterprise is so greatly developed you would scarcely suppose such wreck of property had ever occurred, so entirely have the traces of ruinous war disappeared.

On the 15th of November, 1864, we left this notable city. For two and a half months we had occupied it, built some extensive fortifications, and, as remarked, were free from many of the actual annoyances that usually obtain in time of active hostilities. We were quite fresh, and ready for any emergency that the fortunes of war should provide. It has often occurred to me since the war, if any necessity of civil life should demand of the average citizen a feat of pedestrianism involving a journey of three hundred miles or more, why, the reflection would be painful, and nearly everyone would revolt at the idea of such an undertaking. Yet the men who composed Sherman's army not only regarded it with complacency, but thought a huge tramp of a thousand miles to

Richmond among the possibilities of the campaign. And, sure enough, not only compassed that, but actually marched to Washington City, and were encamped there six months after leaving Atlanta, having taken Savannah, Columbia, Fayetteville, Raleigh, Goldsboro, and Joe Johnston's army. After reducing Atlanta almost to a heap of ruins, we took our leave of the devoted city, the conflagration of the burning city being visible for two or three nights after we left it. We went by Stone Mountain, where the troops stopped long enough to effectually destroy the railroad, something they had become very expert at, and everywhere the army touched, this indiscriminate destruction went on. The weather was fine, and I do not now recall a single rainy day. The roads were excellent, and the artillery and teams kept pace with the marching column without difficulty. The country was well stocked with all kinds of provisions. The corn was gathered, and the sweet potatoes, that were everywhere abundant, "started from the ground," and seemed to bid us welcome to the sacred soil of Georgia. Cattle, sheep, hogs and poultry abounded, and a continual picnic and "feast of fat things" greeted us everywhere. The colored people appreciated our presence, but the disloyal whites, where they presumed to give us an audience at all, looked on us and our operations with grim despair depicted on their countenances. Many of them fled from their homes, or hid themselves till the army passed by, when it is likely most of them returned. Many of the negroes thought "the year of Jubilee had come," and struck out and marched to the sea with us. Some few of them were loyal to and preferred to stay and share the fate of their masters.

At one place where I was superintending the loading of some wagons with corn, the escort of men had scattered so as to make me uneasy for fear of capture; I wanted to hurry up the loading and get back on the road the troops were marching on as soon as possible. I got a revolver and went to the plantation hands and demanded their help to load the corn. With a great display of ivory they indicated their reluctance. When I made a brandish of the pistol they went to work, one of them remarking, "it was hard enough to take massa's corn 'thout making his niggas help load it." I did not stop to discuss the ethics of the question with him, but told him he must work hard and keep his mouth shut or we would take him too, which caused him to redouble diligence, and I soon got away. These were the only ones that I saw that indicated affectionate loyalty to their masters. There was another colored man named Ben, who came to us at Atlanta and drove one of the headquarters teams of the 20th corps. His wife, Sally, cooked for one of the officers, mess. They had always been slaves, but elated at the thought of freedom, they started out with the army. Their family, it appears, had been taken away from them, so they did not know anything about them. When the freed men began to flock to our camps, old Aunt Sally would scrutinize them very closely to see if any of them were her children, and inquire for any clue whereby she might hear of them or perchance find them. She said that ten years before they had taken her darter, a girl eight years old, down in what she called the lower country, and I allow she is some whar down thar yet. Her interest and inquiry was so intense that a good many of the soldiers knew about it. I thought, however, as it had been so long, and slaves were bought and sold so frequently and taken from state to state, it was like looking for a needle in a haystack. But when we had got pretty well down towards Savannah a young man and his wife came in to cast their lot with us, or "go to Massa Linkum," as they called it. This man's name was Joe, and some one who knew Aunt Sally and had heard of her great desire to find her daughter, heard Joe address his wife as Nan, ran over to where Sally was cooking supper for her mess, and told her that a young man and woman was camping near them and he heard the man say Nan to his wife, and he thought it might be her girl. The old auntie threw down her cooking utensils and raised her hands and said "de Lord be praised, I know its her," and flew to where they were. Joe, of course, did not have any knowledge of her, and perhaps the girl had forgotten her mother, and as they saw her making toward them they just stared at her and wondered what was the matter. The sight of them checked her somewhat and to assure herself she began to make inquiries about them, "whar dey war from and how long dey libed thar." Nan said she lived about thar, she reckoned, 'bout ten year. She was born up de country near Atlanta, and when she war little her massa had fetched her down thar. The old auntie could not stand it any longer, she just screamed, "uan's is my chile, I knows uan's is; I'se looked for you all de way down, an' bless de good Lord, he's sent uan's to me." The girl, too, recognized her mother and in a little while they were in each others arms, embracing and kissing and shedding of tears, and slapping each other on the back accompanied with joyous screams, raised a commotion in the camp. The soldiers, hard as they seemed to be, were wonderfully moved when they knew what it all meant. Then Ben came and the scene was repeated, all three hugging together and jumping up and down till they seemed exhausted. It was the most powerful demonstration of human emotion I ever saw; some laughed and others cried as they witnessed these exuberances of joy at finding each other again. Aunty was so nearly overcome that she nearly forgot the supper she had so hastily left. It was scantier than usual and very late, but the officer, when he knew what had detained her and made his supper less in quantity, readily forgave her.

CHAPTER IX.

Millidgeville, the capital of Georgia, was occupied by our command without opposition. Gov. Brown and other notables fleeing in great haste. We rested two days here and gave the people a little time to get acquainted with us. Some of them had heard Jeff Davis promise that Hood would soon drive Sherman out of Georgia. They must have lost faith in Jeff and the cause altogether, for certainly they were a blank-looking set of people, never dreaming that the hated Yankees would ever invade their noble domain. But here we were in the heart of the confederacy, at the capital of Georgia and not an armed confederate to dispute our passage, and we were having all our own way. Their senators and members of congress and some of the confederate generals made frantic appeals to be firm, to rally, to destroy their provisions, burn their bridges, fell the trees, blockade the roads, and in every way possible impede the progress of the ruthless invaders. These appeals amounted to very little, all able-bodied men were already in their army, and were doing what they could. Verily Sherman was playing them a huge Yankee caper, beyond their genius and ability to obviate, and we were crushing through the heart of the south, their armies tied up at Nashville and Richmond, and powerless to interfere with the operations of the sagacious Sherman. Many amusing things occurred in the foraging operations. Every available vehicle was brought into requisition as a means of transportation, from the big Kentucky scooped shaped wagon to two wheeled carts or gigs. The old style family carriage was frequently loaded with flour, meal, sweet potatoes, meat and poultry with perhaps fodder on top, and the driver riding one of the animals, which was frequently a cow and a mule yoked together, rope harness and a corn husk collar, making a most ludicrous appearance. (It is not unusual to see a mule and cow hitched to a wagon or farm cart, and a family going to market or to visit friends in such a rig in these days; such a comical sight I witnessed at Ringgold, Ga., the summer of 1895.) When we left Milliegeville we encountered no opposition. Kilpatrick's cavalry had a brush with Wheeler's troops once or twice, but the rebels kept out of the way of our infantry. In a few days we came to Millen where our prisoners were kept, a place almost as notorious as Andersonville. The prison pen was a huge stockade containing ten or twenty acres, a small creek running through it, but not swampy like Andersonville, so the water privilege was some better. The prisoners were compelled to erect houses or sheds for their own shelter. The material was soon all worked up and the later arrivals could not do any better than to scoop holes in the sand, and many of them died and were left, as it were, actually in graves of their own digging. As we approached, the prisoners were moved farther south into Florida, and finally the confederates were so reduced they could not hold them any longer, and they were just turned loose to do the best they could for themselves and find their way to our lines. I had time to make a hasty examination of Millen, and saw several corpses of the poor men in the burrows they had dug in the earth. I sought for some kind of a relic, but it was the barest spot of earth I ever saw. The trees and stumps and roots to the smallest fiber had been dug out for fuel, not a rag or a button or even a chip could be found, as if it had been swept and garnished for every thing that could be utilized for human comfort or subsistence. We thought it was no vandalism to reduce to ashes this prison pen that had been the scene of so much privation and suffering on the part of our prisoners, and soon flames of fire were playing havoc with every available part of this horrid place.

As we drew near to Savannah there were evidences of opposition. Some earthworks were thrown up, trees were felled across the roads, and we got a glimpse of some of the enemy. They did not stop to defend the hastily constructed rifle pits, and evidently thought the last ditch was a little farther on, till finally all the Confederate forces were within the immediate defenses of Savannah. As long as the army was in motion, making twelve or fifteen miles a day, the country furnished plenty of meat and breadstuffs; but when we came near to Savannah and were detained a few days our supplies became exhausted. We had driven large herds of cattle before us, and had a supply of meat sufficient for a number of days, but sweet potatoes were exhausted, and we had not yet communicated with the fleet to draw from it any supplies. However, we were in the rice-growing region, which had just been harvested, and thousands of acres of it stood in the shock. It made good forage for the animals, and when we could find it threshed and hulled it took the place of bread. But rice alone is very light diet, and men in active service need food of a more substantial character. The negroes had hand mortars for hulling it, and the soldiers, when they became stinted for bread, procured these, and for several days prepared rice this way for their own use, which was very tedious, indeed.

Soon the steam threshing and hulling mills were set to work, and the army was mainly supplied with it in proper condition for cooking. I heard one man tell how he made out with the scant ration that he was compelled to hull and cleanse by hand before cooking. "Well," he said, "it takes me about all day to beat the stuff and clean it in order to get enough for one meal, but I arrange to have supper late, then go to bed, and am asleep before I have time to get hungry. Then in the morning I'm as hungry as a bitch wolf that's been in a snowdrift twenty-four hours." But this was only a short experience. The 10th of December we closely invested Savannah, and Sherman demanded its surrender of the rebel commander, who declined. On the 21st it was evacuated, and soon we were all receiving the usual government allowance of hard bread, salt pork and other rations, brought by our fleet. Savannah was not much the worse for Union occupation. As Sherman did not expect to stay long, the inhabitants were interrupted in their business and possessions but very little. And soon business was transacted, stores and shops opened, and peaceable relations were restored in a fair degree. Church bells rang out on the Sabbath, and the worshipers attended as if no ruthless invader had invested this important Confederate seaport. A vast amount of cotton and stores and cannon, with munitions, fell into our hands. Oysters were plenty, and at times these were issued to the soldiers, in the shell, with other rations. I found a rebel photographer, who accepted the results of war, and was so far reconstructed as to be glad to take small photographs at the rate of ten dollars per dozen in "greenbacks." I got a half dozen, for which I paid the modest sum of five dollars. One of these I still have in my possession, which I esteem highly as a relic of the war.

We remained about a month in Savannah, and much enjoyed the semi-tropical climate; the beautiful live oaks, that retain their deep green foliage all winter, with the Spanish moss, in large tresses, hanging perpendicularly from the branches, are very beautiful; flowers of every hue, blooming in mid-winter; the mosquito, with his delicate humming sound, seeking the blood of his unsuspecting victims. These were rendered duly impressive to the men whose esthetical qualities had not been altogether blunted by the stern vicissitudes of "grim-visaged war." Savannah is a city of historic associations. During the Revolutionary war the British seized it and held it three and a half years. The Americans, with their French allies, endeavored to wrest it from them, but were sorely repulsed, and it remained in British hands until nearly the close of the war. Here the noble Pulaski, a Polish count, lost his life, and a beautiful monument has been erected to his memory by the citizens of Savannah. As I gazed upon this imposing monument I seemed scarcely to realize it was possible for me to walk upon the sacred soil where our fathers had shed their blood for liberty and independence, and thus had secured a government based on freedom and equal rights. And now, in less than a hundred years, find a people who had entered on so grand a heritage determined to destroy their blood-bought legacy and render nugatory the great sacrifices of their fathers, to whom they built this substantial monument. Yet so it was, and I, a member of Sherman's army, representing the principles of Pulaski, with others, were engaged in the awful acts of war, to conserve these interests and principles from the disloyal attempts of these misguided people.

CHAPTER X.

On the 27th of January, 1865, Sherman's forces were moving in an active campaign, his object being to put his army where he could co-operate with Grant in an active campaign, which would certainly result in the complete overthrow of the rebellion. He preferred to march the army through the Carolinas rather than to take shipping and move by water to Virginia; and he rightly judged, if such a march could be made, it would greatly cripple the resources of the enemy and cause the evacuation of Charleston, Wilmington, and perhaps other places on the Atlantic seaboard, which would be an irreparable loss to the Confederacy. The floods of the Savannah river prevented the crossing of all the troops, the pontoon breaking before they were all over, and part of them, with the wagon trains, were compelled to march up the river, on the Georgia side, and cross at Sister's Ferry, which they did with great difficulty, and formed a junction with the rest of the army that had marched up on the South Carolina side of the river. The Confederates apparently never thought of such a move being made in the dead of winter, and Sherman so adroitly disguised his object in threatening Augusta, Charleston and Columbia at the same time that they could not guess his objective. Hence, there was no concentration of their forces to ward off his advance from any of these places. Sherman was thus able to get his army to Columbia and beyond before they could have any idea of his real object. Thus Columbia fell into our hands without any serious opposition. The railroads were destroyed, and the country was stripped of everything that could be of any service to the enemy. It seemed that supplies were amply sufficient while the army was in motion, for, as on the march to the sea, we were depending largely upon the country for forage and provisions, having the same orders to take everything needful for the support of man and beast. I suppose that South Carolina, naturally being the poorer state, could not furnish the lavish supply we had found in Georgia, but as it was not intended to spend any more time than necessary, we were not at all stinted in the matter of supplies. One feature of the country was the great extent of pine woods, of the pitch variety, and, in time of peace, the seat of the tar and turpentine industry. On the line of march, for miles, were trees that had been tapped for turpentine. The process of tapping is by an instrument like a gouge, cutting across one side of the trunk of the tree, from the ground as high as they could reach. This causes the sap or turpentine to flow, and run down the place so gouged, where it is caught in vessels set for it. When the tree begins to show exhaustion, or the season becomes late, the liquid congeals and forms a crust of pure resin. When we passed through nearly all the trees had this crust of resin on them; when we were marching at night these were fired, and for hours would burn and light up the woods with thousands of torches, many of them burning nearly all night. Some of the trees were dead and full of pitch, and would burn from the root to the top, presenting a wonderful illumination, a night march being as easily accomplished as though it were daylight. A large tar factory and warehouse, in which a large amount of tar and resin was stored away, was fired by the troops. There was such a vast amount that it became very liquid, and ran a stream. Like water seeking its level, it flowed into and on the surface of a small stream, carrying the flames of fire, so that it actually formed a stream of flame that was wonderful to behold.

The weather was more unfavorable than on the "March to the Sea." It rained a great deal, so the quicksand soon cut through, and the mules and horses would mire down, being extricated with difficulty. One of the teams belonging to headquarters, and driven by a man named Kelly, got stuck, just as Gen. Sherman and staff were passing. The old general, who was a close observer of things, concluded that the driver was not doing what he could to extricate his team. As the accident was delaying the marching column, he expostulated with the driver, and wanted to know if he could not do better than that. Kelly recognized the general, and said: "Yes, Uncle Billy, if you will give me a chew of tobacco I will get them out before you can say 'scat,' for I ain't had any for two or three days." The general seemed somewhat taken back by this appeal, but said: "Orderly," addressing one of his escort, "give that man some tobacco," which he did. Kelly bit off a large quid, and began to chew vigorously; then cracked his whip, and the mules straightened out, pulling the load safely out of the quagmire. The old general smiled curiously, and rode away without saying anything. It became necessary to corduroy the roads, which was done by throwing the rails of the worm fences into the road, when these happened to be at hand, and, in case there were no fences, the pioneers cut timbers and filled the road with them. It was very rough and jolted fearfully, but it was much better than miring in the sand. At the battles of Averysboro and Bentonville our wounded had to be carried in ambulances and wagons over these rough, corduroyed places, which was a painful operation to some of them, and frequently their screams were appalling to hear. We had a great many considerable streams to cross, as the Great and Little Pedees, Catawba, Cape Fear and Santee rivers. These were all crossed by the use of the pontoon, the rebels having burned all the bridges. This, however, delayed us but very little; they might as well have left them, and they would have been serviceable to them in only a few weeks afterwards, when their armies were disbanded and they had to return to peaceable pursuits again. There is no doubt but what the South lost as much property by their own vandalism in destroying it, to prevent its falling into our hands, as we did to prosecute the war and bring them to terms, so they ought not to charge all the destruction of property to the Yankees when they applied the torch so frequently themselves.

In this stage of the campaign our foraging operations became more complicated. The Confederates were centralizing their forces to resist us, and some of the more venturesome of the runners were captured and some of them were shot. Two of our regiment were captured. They had secured what they could conveniently take care of, mainly poultry, cured meat and sweet potatoes, and, sitting down to await the arrival of the advance guard, concluded to while away the time by a game of cards. They became intensely interested, and before they were aware of it a squad of Wheeler's men swooped down upon them and made them prisoners. They took their arms from them and divested them of their plunder, and soon they were in the rebel lines. J. W. Alford, of our company, was one of them. His companion was a recruit of Company F, named George Ham, who had not been long with us. The Confederates were still retreating before us. One night as they were marching, these prisoners were in charge of cavalry, but they were on foot, with a squad before them and two horsemen behind them. Alford, feeling his shoe had become loose, stopped and stooped over to tie it, and was agreeably surprised to see his guards ride by without observing him. He stood stock still for a minute, and then darted out of the road into the woods and hid in a hollow tree, remaining all night and the next day, during which time he witwitnessed the bulk of the rebel army march by, which he regarded with breathless anxiety. The next morning early he heard the tramp of a marching column, and, to his great delight, the men were clothed in blue and carried the stars and stripes. He lost no time in making himself known, and soon found his way back to his own regiment, having been gone only a few days. Ham did not fare so well. He was sent South, and finally, when the Confederacy was entirely used up, he found his way to our lines, in Florida, but never got back to the regiment until we reached Washington City.

From Columbia we moved on Cheraw, on Great Pedee river, near the North Carolina line. Here we found a bonanza of good things awaiting us. The citizens of Charleston had sent to this place their high wines, and Brussels carpet, and much finery and provision, which they thought would escape the "fell destroyer" by being so far in the interior, and lo! it was right in the way of the great army as it wormed its way through the hotbed of secession, as South Carolina was frequently termed. At Cheraw twenty-five cannon and a magazine of powder were captured, but, unfortunately, the powder was blown up, by accident, killing and wounding a number of men. We then marched on Fayetteville. The Confederates, now comprehending the nature of our movement, began to mass their forces to resist our progress as much as possible. The remnant of Hood's army, Hardee's Savannah garrison, besides the troops of other deserted positions, made considerable of an army, but were still unable to cope with the victorious and jubilant veterans of Sherman. We occupied Fayetteville, a very fine city, where there was a large arsenal, that was formerly United States property. This was completely destroyed, but the city was unharmed, as far as I saw. A great many rebels deserted and came into our lines, who were very anxious to see the end of the struggle, being satisfied it was useless to contend any longer against the Government. It seemed that we could see the beginning of the end. My regiment had now marched nearly a thousand miles through the enemy's best country, yet had not sustained a single casualty by the enemy's guns. In fact, we had not had a man killed or wounded since the battle of Peach Tree Creek, where the lamented Young was taken off the field mortally wounded. We were now in North Carolina. The soldiers seemed to have more respect for property, and were more moderate in prosecuting warlike operations than when we were burrowing through South Carolina. The men took a fiendish delight in making the people of the latter state feel the iron hand of war, because South Carolina was the first to revolt and secede, and somehow, thus far, had been signally free from the tread of hostile armies. But now her cup was full, and she drank to the dregs the wrath of the Union defenders. When we came into North Carolina foraging was less rigid, and but few acts that could be construed as vandalism occurred. Just before we entered North Carolina I was attracted by seeing a number of men besieging the door of a negro cabin, situated on a large plantation. As there seemed to be something unusual going on, I concluded to satisfy my curiosity. The cabin was very small, and a man six feet high could scarcely have stood erect in it. A large, corpulent colored woman, who was sweating profusely, had been prevailed upon to cook hoe cake for the boys. She had just finished one, and there was a somewhat angry dispute going on between two of the men as to who had the best right to it, as it seemed everyone took their turn. I had that morning picked up a cavalryman's plume, bright and new in appearance, and stuck it in my forage cap, and had forgotten all about it. As I came up, it was evident the old auntie did not know who should have the cake, and was perhaps a little out of patience with their strife. Seeing my plume, she thought I was some person of distinction, so she told the boys, who were waxing warm in the dispute, she would not "gib it any one ob dem; she would gib it to de captin dar," and tossed it over to me. Of course I appreciated this mark of substantial respect, and expressed my thanks with becoming suavity. I would have been willing to have been considered even a major-general if that would have taken the cake. When I beat a hasty retreat I heard one of the disappointed men say: "You fool wench, that is no captain; he isn't any better than we are." This letting me down in the estimation of the old auntie was of no consequence to me, as I had the prize and was not disposed to make any explanations.

On another occasion my messmate (whose name was Berry), and I found a good, fat shoat, and a minie ball from my gun brought the poor animal down. We were both busily engaged taking off the hide, when an elderly man, very dignified in appearance, came suddenly upon us. We both saw him about the same time, and looked at each other but did not look up, continuing our work silently. Soon he spoke, and said: "Well, gentlemen, how's this?" Berry, essaying to be spokesman, said: "How's what?" "Why," said he, "that is my hog, and I gave no orders to you or any one else to kill it." "Well, captain, (Berry always called strangers captain), we are Sherman's bummers, down here in South Carolina putting down the rebel lion, and we have orders to 'forage liberally off the country.' We have not had any meat for some time, and we will take this to camp and divide with the rest of the boys as far as it will go. It's all right, isn't it?" "Well, no," said he; "I deserve some consideration on the part of Sherman's men. I am not disloyal. I served the United States as an officer in the Mexican war, and I ought to know something about military regulations, so I enter my solemn protest against this way of doing, and want it stopped." "Well, Cap, you see we've got the hog now, and we can't give it up. Of course we don't know who's loyal and who isn't; we take what we find in South Carolina and ask no questions, for we know everybody's Secesh—never heard anybody deny it but you. It's too bad you're down here among such a set. Now, if it was in North Carolina, I wouldn't wonder a bit about seeing a Union man, but it's too bad, Cap, that you're a kind of an Old Dog Tray among a set of the meanest dogs the Almighty ever let live. I'm awfully sorry for you, but you go to headquarters and tell Uncle Billy about it; like as not he'll pay you for the pig." By this time the pig was dressed, and, dividing it, we each shouldered a piece and returned to camp. We never heard whether the old gentleman took his complaint to headquarters or not, and that was the last we saw of him.

Soon after leaving Fayetteville the Confederates began to indicate serious opposition, and greater care was necessary to conduct the campaign than at any time since leaving Atlanta. Gen. Schofield was at Newbern with the 23d Corps, and had orders to effect a junction with Sherman at Goldsboro; Gen. Terry, with the 10th Corps, was moving up from Wilmington for the same purpose. Both encountered some opposition, but succeeded in carrying out their orders. Our forces had two engagements, one at Averysboro and one at Bentonville. These were the heaviest battles fought since leaving Atlanta. The Confederates were entirely foiled in their attempts to arrest the progress of Sherman or prevent his forming a junction with Schofield's or Terry's armies. There was considerable loss of life in these engagements, but our regiment was fortunate and did not lose a man, although exposed to some severe firing. One of my friends had a close call. A minie ball passed through the coffee pail fastened to his belt, and spoiled it for that service. Several others experienced narrow escapes, and no doubt were thankful it was no worse. The rebel forces hastily retreated, and on the 21st of March we were safely encamped in Goldsboro, with the prospect of a short rest.

CHAPTER XI.

During our occupation of Goldsboro the army was thoroughly refitted. A large number of new recruits came to us, and the veterans drew new clothing. Gen. Mower took command of the 20th Corps, and Slocum's left wing became known as the Army of Georgia. We had scarcely rested twenty days when our active commander put the army in motion towards Raleigh, where the Confederate army, under Joe Johnston, was doing all it could to resist the aggressive operations of Sherman. We were inspired by the hope that very soon the bottom would fall out of what was left of the so-called Southern Confederacy. But we were not prepared for the grand, good news that came to us the next day after leaving Goldsboro. It was so much more than we expected right then. We thought Grant would be unable to capture Lee until we should join him, but we were glad, on the 9th of April, that Lee's army surrendered, and Richmond and Petersburg had fallen into our hands. The whole army went wild with excitement. It looked for awile as if the officers would lose their heads and the army become demoralized with delight. But we hastened on, entering Raleigh April 13th, and Johnston, instead of wanting to fight, proposed an armistice to negotiate the surrender of all the armies of the Confederacy, and thus, at one stroke of the pen, as it were, seal the fate of the Confederacy forever. In the midst of our rejoicing over the fate of Lee's army, and during the truce with Johnston, came the sad news of the assassination of President Lincoln and the murderous assault on Secretary Seward, which was appalling to the army, who had come to regard Mr. Lincoln as one of the greatest and best of men. It was charged by many soldiers that it was a plot concocted by Jeff Davis and his chief counselors, but this was in the heat of excitement, and it is probable this conspiracy originated with Booth, the assassin of Lincoln, who was an intense sympathizer with the rebellion, and, infatuated by an inordinate desire for notoriety, took this method to gratify his demoniacal ambition. As summary vengeance overtook him and his confederates, it largely mollified the army, and they became resigned to the sad fate of their beloved president; but still many contended for the capital punishment of Jeff Davis to avenge the death of Lincoln. After the army had recovered from the stunning effects of this calamity and their grief had become somewhat assuaged, the men sung "We'll Hang

Jeff Davis to a Sour Apple Tree," with a vengeful vehemence that would have made the rebel chief terror-stricken had he heard it. But the arch conspirator was destined to go unpunished (save his political disabilities), and he was not hung, even to a sweet apple tree, and actually found an asylum, for the remainder of his days, in the country he tried to destroy and under the flag he sought to blot out of existence, which may be regarded as questionable magnanimity, and a travesty on justice without a precedent in the history of civil government.

The first terms agreed on by Sherman and Johnston were conditioned on the endorsement or rejection of the government at Washington; therefore the cartel was sent there for action upon it. It was rejected by the government, as conceding too much that was favorable to the South, and involving some political points that Sherman should not have considered, as an army commander, as his jurisdiction was purely of a military character. So the truce ended, and we prepared to move on the enemy. We actually begun the march, when Johnston, knowing the cause was lost, and that he was unable to cope with Sherman's forces, asked for another truce, and on the 26th of April, 1865, surrendered his army, on terms similar to those given by Grant to Lee, and thus the war was virtually at an end, and the dawn of peace, sweet peace was upon us. The effect of this upon the army was very exhilarating indeed. Strong men wept for joy, and some even hugged each other and gave way to every manifestation of delight. Military discipline was so relaxed for a time that I was actually fearful of the result. In their exuberance of joy, the boys could not restrain their delight in perpetrating practical jokes, some of which were very rough, and even dangerous. One that was often played was when a comrade was caught asleep in the daytime, to put a small charge of powder in a canteen and stealthily place it under the head of the sleeper, or as near as possible, but under ground a little, and then ignite the powder. This, of course, would destroy the canteen, but otherwise no damage was done, more than to give the sleeper a good shaking up. This was played quite frequently, and I never knew of any one being hurt, but several got very angry. I never took a hand in anything of that kind, regarding it as too dangerous. Finally the officers put a stop to it. Our camp at Raleigh was near the North Carolina insane hospital, and the soldiers were forbidden to interfere in any way with it. But the inmates would come to the windows and sometimes greatly amuse us with their actions and conversation. One day a patient threw out of a window a letter directed to Gen. Sherman. It was reported to be a very well written communication, indicating the perfect sanity of the writer. It contained a good knowledge of the military situation and the principles involved in the struggle. The writer stated that he was a Union man, and when secession was attempted, his father and brother, being ardent supporters of the Confederacy, persecuted him for his political principles, and had trumped up the charge of insanity against him, having him incarcerated in the asylum. He had languished there during the whole period of the war. This was presented so clear and plausible that it was investigated. Some of the surgeons of the army were sent and permitted to see the man, but whether they were honestly dealt with or not I cannot say. They reported they found no one capable of writing such a letter, and the solution, I judge, will ever remain one of the mysteries of the war.

A grand review of our corps was given in Raleigh, many of the citizens looking on, I suppose, with a good degree of suppressed indignation, as we were their conquerors, and they could not have regarded it otherwise than a kind of crowing over our success and their complete downfall and humiliation. But we did not distress them long with our presence, for before the close of April we began our march to the Potomac. The march to Washington was by way of Richmond, and enabled us to pass over nearly all the ground of active operations between Grant's and Lee's armies, which was quite interesting. Appomattox and the surrounding country still contained fresh evidences of what had occurred there, and we were sufficiently experienced in the art of war to understand what had been done. One place, Grant's army, in order to move light and successfully pursue the Confederates, had destroyed some of their personal effects, as blankets and overcoats, and we saw many of these that had escaped total destruction by fire, but nothing remained that could be of any service to anyone. We frequently met groups of Lee's paroled men, returning to their homes, who were in a pitiable condition, without money and without anything to eat, their government a complete wreck, and no one of their friends able to help them. They were in great want for proper clothing, and they must have been reduced to the greatest possible straits before they were able to procure any, for the whole land was impoverished and desolate. When they reached their homes, many of them must have found them destroyed and deserted, and their friends scattered. They were usually free to tell their needs, and it was an interesting sight to see our soldiers divide their rations with them, and, as much, as possible, mitigate their privations, bidding them God-speed in their homeward journey. Their need was so great that on several occasions our commissary department issued rations to them the same as to our own men. The great commander of our armies had shown his thoughtfulness of their need by allowing every person to retain their horses or mules, where they were claimed as personal property, remarking that "they would need them for raising a crop." This spirit largely prevailed through the army, and now that the Confederacy was defunct and all their armies disbanded, there seemed no resentment lurking in the hearts of their captors, and nearly all wished their late antagonists might soon enjoy the blessings of peace and plenty. I suppose but few other regiments saw more of the territory of the Confederacy than ours, for we had seen service on both sides of the Mississippi; as low down as Vicksburg, in Kentucky, East and West Tennessee, Alabama, Georgia and both the Carolinas, and now, as spectators, we were viewing nearly all the theatre of operations of our comrades of the Potomac army. Our marches would probably aggregate three thousand miles. By the 9th of May we were in Richmond, and rested a few days. I was privileged to see a great deal of the city, and visited some points of interest, as the State House and Libby Prison, which had now ceased forever to be a place of incarceration of United States soldiers, as prisoners. There were still the grim evidences of what had taken place there during the four years of hostilities. I felt gratified to realize that no more those dingy walls would shut out the light of day and the pure air of heaven from the brave defenders of our glorious Union. I beheld with pleasure the imposing equestrian statue of Washington, and the bronze figures of Patrick Henry, Thomas Jefferson, John Marshall, and other noted Virginians, that had escaped the vandalism of the Confederates when they evacuated the city. The ruthless destruction of property by the rebels at this stage of the war is inexcusable. It did not, in any sense, disparage the government at Washington, and was a destructive loss inflicted on themselves and which they would have to make good in the near future. They must have known by this time that the United States would establish its supremacy all over the land, and that their cause and confederacy was hopelessly lost.

I saw St. John's Episcopal Church, made famous by the meeting of the Virginia convention, in 1775, in which Patrick Henry made his celebrated speech, ending with the sentence, "Give me Liberty or give me Death." It was the 11th or 12th of May we bid farewell to Richmond and started to Washington, D. C. The 20th Corps went by the way of Spottsylvania and Chancellorsville. The grim evidences of battle were abundant at Spottsylvania, although it was about a year since the sanguinary conflict there. The court house was standing, in a dilapidated condition, many cannon balls having gone through it. The several lines of breastworks were visible, and the trees were scarred and broken by shot and shell. Hundreds of skeletons of men and horses were scattered over the ground, some of the poor men who had been hastily buried shallow. The rains had washed them almost bare again. Some had been laid behind logs and covered with bark, in some instances the bare skull or feet protruding, and many others were lying on the ground just where they had met their death. For more than a half-day's march these ghastly scenes greeted our eyes. The government, as soon as possible, gathered up these precious remains of its fallen heroes, and they now rest, though unknown, in the National Cemetery on Arlington Heights. Many regiments of our corps had formerly served in the Potomac army, and were engaged in the disastrous battle of Chancellorsville. Of course they knew the ground quite well, and the recollection of their retreat from Stonewall Jackson's men was quite vivid. Here it was that the brave Gen. Howard vainly tried to rally the 11th Corps, but they were panic-stricken, and the whole army retired, having sustained a disastrous defeat.

CHAPTER XII.

We came to the vicinity of Alexandria the 18th of May, and went into camp. At this place we saw the hotel where the lamented Ellsworth was shot, in the act of pulling down a secession flag, early in 1861. We also passed near Mt. Vernon, the Washington estate, where the Father of his Country is buried. We went hurriedly by, and had to satisfy our curiosity by a mere glimpse of it as we passed. At Alexandria we were detained till the occasion of the grand review, the 23d and 24th of May. Meade's Army of the Potomac passed in review the 23d, and was witnessed by thousands of admiring and patriotic spectators, including many distinguished foreigners, belonging to the diplomatic service. The 24th Sherman's army passed in review, and the same mass of people regarded them with patriotic delight. The foragers were represented in full force, with the accompaniment of negroes, mules, with chickens and pigs and other kinds of captured trophies that were incident to the March to the Sea and the campaign through the Carolinas. We were the "observed of all observers," and this feature of the review was tremendously cheered by the enthusiastic multitude. We passed through Washington, and camped within the limits of Bladensburg, Maryland, which may be regarded as a suburb of Washington, although it is not in the District of Columbia. For two weeks we remained in this camp, and, the war being practically ended, military discipline was considerably relaxed, the soldiers enjoying the freedom of the city, with almost entire suspension from military duty. I visited the Capitol building, the White House, or Presidential mansion, the Smithsonian Institute, with its vast collection of scientific specimens and natural curiosities, the Treasury building and the Patent office, with its vast array of ingenious devices, representing the inventive talent of the great American nation, and a vast collection of relics gathered from every part of the country, and some of them dating back to the discovery of America. Among these was Washington's military camp chest and contents; set of chinaware, sword, and some of his uniform; saddle and spurs; beautiful bedspread, said to have been woven by Martha Washington; also Gen. Jackson's uniform and sword which he wore in the battle of New Orleans, and many other things. Congress was not in session, but the Capitol was open, and the Union defenders were permitted to see all they could that pertained to the great government they had saved by their valor in four years of unprecedented sanguinary conflict. I was at the White House and sat awhile in the reception room, but did not see the President nor any of his family that day, but saw him afterwards, driving in his carriage. Grant, Sherman, and nearly all the noted Union Generals I had seen frequently, so that it had ceased to be a novelty. Gen. Grant was the only general that I ever had the honor of speaking to. I was one day drawing water at a well, near Rossville, Georgia, shortly after the battle of Missionary Ridge, November, 1863, when he and his staff stopped for a drink. I passed the General a tin cup of water, which he drank, thanking me kindly. I then inquired if he had got entirely well from the accident he had a number of weeks before, by his horse falling with him. He thanked me again, and said he thought he was quite well. I was only twenty years old at the time, and felt very proud to be spoken to by the man whom I have always regarded as the greatest military genius that ever lived; I was very much pleased, and I think he was pleased also to have one of his private soldiers indicate solicitude for his welfare. Since I have read Gen. Grant's Memoirs I feel that I know him, as a man, a great deal better and have a greater insight into his heart, which, if I had possessed at that time, I could have approached the great man with a good deal less restraint than I did.

These two weeks of rest and pleasurable recreation soon passed by, and on the 7th of June, 1865, my twenty-second natal day, we went through the formality of muster out of the United States service, but to draw pay up to the time of arrival at state rendezvous. The next day we left Washington, the other regiments of our brigade turning out in large force to bid us good-bye. These were the 31st Wisconsin, 143d New York, 61st and 82d Ohio, and 82d Illinois. We had been associated with them in active campaign ever since October, 1863, and had marched from Bridgeport, Alabama, by way of Chattanooga, Atlanta, Savannah, Columbia, Raleigh and Richmond, to Washington, nearly two thousand miles, fighting many bloody battles, and sweeping majestically through the enemy's country. They sent up hearty cheers and waved their caps, which salute we likewise returned, as the token of final adieu. We parted forever. I never met any of them since, except one man who was a member of the 82d Ohio. His name is A. Rose and his residence Eddyville, Iowa. We marched to the depot, where we boarded a train of open coal cars, the best transportation they could give us then, which of course was a considerable improvement on the past method of locomotion by which we had rendered such effective service in crushing the rebellion. In the language of one of the boys: "Well, these are rough cars—no seats, no shelter—but it beats tramping all hollow." It rained a good deal, but the weather was warm, and we experienced little inconvenience from it. It was 2:00 p. m. before we were fairly on the way from Washington. The people at the towns and stations and even country places would wave their handkerchiefs and hats and cheer us as we passed along, evidently glad that the war was over, and the regime of blood and destruction brought to a close. As night came on we had to eat our suppers without coffee, and make our sleeping couches as best we could in the uncomfortable and crowded cars. But by daylight next morning our government, thoughtful of our need, had arranged for a soldiers' sumptuous repast at Cumberland, Maryland, where we found many barrels of coffee, hot and strong in aromatous flavor, to which we had free access. Soft bread and boiled meat in abundance for everyone to help themselves. I do not recall eating a more refreshing meal during the war than when I broke my fast at Cumberland. After all had eaten, the train again sped on, the railway running mainly through a mountainous region, crossing streams and frightful gorges that made one dizzy to gaze upon. The people cheered along the way, as they had done the day before, to which we made suitable acknowledgement as we passed along. By night we arrived at Parkersburg, West Virginia, where we left the cars, just beyond the city limits. In a wooded field, we went into camp for the night. Next morning, bright and early, we marched through the city and embarked on a steamboat, the C. T. Dumont, a very fine craft, and large enough to accomodate and make comfortable the entire regiment. The day was beautiful, and our enraptured souls were thrilled with delight in viewing the beautiful landscapes of Kentucky on one side and Ohio on the other, many expressions escaping the lips of the men, accordingly as they were impressed. One heard more frequently was: "Well, that's something like; that's the land of the free, the home of the brave. That's God's country! Hurrah! Hurrah!" We were somewhat hindered by the stage of low water, and several places the boat could not float over the bars. Then the boat would land and the troops disembark and walk round the shallow water, which made the trip somewhat monotonous. But beautiful grass lands prevailed, studded here and there with mulberry trees, and the fruit, ripe and luscious, hung temptingly on the branches. Some of the men, expert in climbing, were soon aloft, making way with it, and throwing down large quantities to their comrades, and thus consumed valuable time. The boat would pass the shoal, and toot, and ring the bell, while the men, bent on enjoying the mulberries, were strung away back almost to where the boat had left them, and, in the most laggardly way, coming on board again, which was very exasperating to the commander of the boat, who indulged in some profanity, and threatened to leave without them if they did not hurry. But finally all got on board, and some of the boys joked the captain, by way of complimenting him on his great accommodation in stopping and allowing them to go ashore for refreshments. This soon put the jolly tar in good humor, and he laughed and seemed to enjoy the pleasantry as much as any of us. That afternoon we passed Cincinnati, and by twilight we were at Lawrenceburg, Indiana, where we left the boat, and were there to take the cars for Camp Butler, near Springfield, Illinois. At Lawrenceburg we met with a grand reception. The citizens and patriotic ladies had arranged to give us a good supper at their own expense. They had most delicious coffee, sweet rusk bread, pies and cakes, and other viands that are peculiar to the highest form of civilization. Butter for our bread, cream for our coffee, boiled ham, in thin slices, and generous cuts of roast beef, were bounteously bestowed upon us. We stood in line, and beautiful young ladies, with loaded trays, passed up and down, serving us, apparently taking great delight in showing substantial hospitality to the returning veterans, who had braved the innumerable perils of an awful war and secured the supremacy of our noble government. I am told these generous and patriotic people of Lawrenceburg gave a like reception to all the troops that passed that way, returning to their homes from the seat of war. I have always had a feeling of gratitude, approximating reverence, for their patriotism and unparalleled generosity on that occasion. We left them soon after dispatching their toothsome viands, cheering them, as the best way of making our acknowledgements, as we took the train and departed on the homeward journey. His Excellency, Gov. Oglesby, of Illinois, had provided regular passenger cars for the remainder of the trip, as we had been nearly overcome with the kindness of the people of Lawrenceburg. We were sensibly impressed to behold these comfortable cars and to know it was arranged by the providence of our excellent governor, who was also a soldier, and had the marks of rebel lead upon his person. We felt that we were heroes, indeed, and appreciated by the people whom we had served, which gave us a feeling of complacency and delight that perhaps is impossible to realize under any other circumstances. It has been said that "Republics are ungrateful.'" Whatever truth may be in the ungracious sentiment, it certainly will not apply to the generation of men and women that comprised the loyal masses of the country during the great rebellion.

It may be that the generation of people that have come on the stage of action since the war, and who have not heartfelt experience of patriotism, fostered by the fearful ordeal of the baptism of blood, for a nation's life, cannot appreciate the old soldier and express the gratitude that is commensurate with patriotic deeds, and the far-reaching results to which they have become the legatees. Be that as it may, I am sure the men and women of the war time were not wanting in gratitude to the "boys in blue," which in innumerable ways was made evident and satisfactory to them, who bore the "brunt of the battle in the heat of the day." The next morning we breakfasted at Indianapolis, the government providing for our entertainment at the soldiers' home. Of course we did not have the delicacies that we had enjoyed at Lawrenceburg, but good coffee, soft bread and boiled meat were abundantly provided for two meals. We had no money, for we had not seen the paymaster since we left Savannah; therefore we could not purchase anything in the way of eatables, no matter how much we craved them. The trains were not cannon ball or lightning express, and the capacity of the roads being greatly taxed in dispatching the veterans to their homes, great care was evidently being taken to prevent accidents; so the time made was only moderate, and we were another day and night on the train before we reached Springfield. On reaching our own State we were much cheered at all the towns and stations, and at many places the people were on the lookout for their own friends and relatives coming home from the war. About midnight of the last night we were on the cars, at one station they were look'ng for the 116th or 117th (I am not certain which), and as they knew they would have to pass through and receive their pay and final discharge at Camp Butler, they had provided a lot of refreshments for the boys. As our train pulled in and they saw it was loaded with soldiers they could not restrain their generosity any longer, and supposing we were their boys, they threw their turkeys, chickens and other dainties through the doors and windows of the cars, never imagining who we were. Most of the men were asleep.

but the novelty of such a shower of good things had a very wakeful tendency, and soon all were wide awake and ready to partake of this unexpected providence. When these happy donors had disposed of all their viands, some of them thought to inquire who we were, and of course we told them we were the 101st. I heard one remark, "O, shaw! we thought you were the 116th; but never mind, it's some of Uncle Sam's boys who've got the treat," and the train moving out, they could not have taken up their victuals if they had desired. About an hour after we left, the train came along bearing the regiment they were looking for, but they had nothing for them. I met some of them the next day, who remarked that it was a good joke, if we did get the benefit of it. I said we thought we had reached God's country, sure enough, to witness a shower of dainties at the midnight hour; and we were not at all wanting in capacity for proper storage of that grade of refreshments.

When we reached Camp Butler tents were provided, and we went into camp. We were informed that it would be several days before we should be paid off. Some of the men were so impatient to reach their homes. They procured some money somehow (a few may have had some) and went to their homes. Of course they had to come back to be paid off and receive their discharges. On June 22nd the paymaster made his appearance. The discharges had all been made out and the amount due each man carefully estimated. So in a short time we were again citizens, and free from all military restraint; a good supply of "greenbacks," enjoying good health and nearly home again. Before we left the camp we listened to the farewell sermon of our chaplain, J. B. Seymour, whose preaching services had been sadly interrupted by the intense activity of Sherman, so that I do not remember hearing a religious discourse since we had left Bridgeport, Ala., about May 1st, 1864. It was just out of personal respect that most of us gave the chaplain a hearing this time, for we judged we should scatter all over the country and scarcely, if ever, see each other again. I don't remember anything about the sermon, but I suppose it was good advice to be followed the residue of our days. Chaplain Seymour entered the active ministry of the Methodist Episcopal church and for many years dispensed the gospel in central Illinois, and a few years ago went to his eternal reward. Governor Oglesby also made an address, the most of which I have forgotten. I recall an allusion to our uniform. He said to not be in a hurry to cast it off, for we had a right to be proud of it. "Yes," said he;

"boys, keep those old, lousy breeches as a memento of the eminent service you have given your country," etc., etc. But the boys had worn the blue a long time, and a change was agreeable to them, and soon they were all rigged up in costumes of the latest improved pattern. Our friends of Jacksonville and Morgan County had hoped to give us a grand reception and dinner on our arrival, but we were not aware of their good intentions; so after obtaining our discharges there was no attempt to hold us together as a military organization, and all took their own time and manner in going from Springfield to their several homes. But the good people were bound to give a reception, which was appointed for next week.

By an evening train I reached Jacksonville, and put up for the night. In the morning I met a number of old friends, whose hearty congratulations were very agreeable. I then procured a livery team, and started for the paternal home. Our people had no knowledge of our return, for they could not tell when the government would pay us off. They expected us, and yet it was a surprise. When I drove into the old farm yard the family had just got up from the dinner table, and mother was the first person to see me as I stepped out of the buggy. I heard her speak my name and announce my arrival. Father had just picked up a newspaper, and, with it in one hand and his spectacles in the other, was soon by the side of mother, both getting to the gate at the same time. Mother claimed her right to embrace me first, and father permitted her to pass through first, and soon a mother's tender kiss was imparted unto me. Father, trembling with emotion, soon grasped me kindly by the hand, and embraced me like I was a child, while my own heart was too full for utterance, and all shed tears of joy. My sister, Martha, and brothers, Harvey and William, were at home, and also took a part in these family greetings, so full of tenderness and delight it is impossible to describe. But that their gratitude and joy at my return was unbounded is a mild way of expressing the feeling of that occasion.

The day appointed for the reception at Jacksonville was a beautiful one, moderately warm for that month, and vast crowds of people assembled to welcome us, and for profuse preparation and intensity of friendly and patriotic feeling this was the most impressive occasion I ever saw. The men were almost all present, and their friends from far and near. Strawn's Hall was engaged for speeches, by distinguished men, and appropriate music. Gov. Yates, who at this time was U. S. Senator, made the principal address, which was highly eulogistic of our services and partook of the jubilant and patriotic spirit that prevailed on account of the war victoriously for the Union. Among other things he referred to the part we took in the "March to the Sea," and, delineating our absolute sway over the territory and property of the confederacy, he made the apt quotation, "You were lords of the fowl and the brute," etc., etc. He also paid his respects to Jeff Davis, the head of the late confederacy, and, in a humorous way, sketched the capture of that worthy, in woman's clothes. "Never," said he, "has anything happened so romantic since the days of Goody Two Shoes and Jack, the Giant Killer," all of which we were in a condition to enjoy hugely. Sheridan's Twenty Miles Away; or, Cedar Creek, was declaimed by an expert, who's name I have forgotten. This was highly applauded, as it was the first time we had heard it. I have listened to it many times since, but never have heard it rendered so impressively as on that occasion; but time and place might have much to do with it. After the exercises at the hall we repaired to the old court-house yard, where there was set the largest table, with the most abundant and varied eatables, I have ever seen. The order was to seat first all the members of the 101st Regiment of Illinois Volunteers; next, all other soldiers of the war who might be present (and there were a great many of them); next, the fathers and mothers, wives, brothers and sisters of the soldiers; last, the promiscuous multitude, which was large, and the larger part of the afternoon was taken up with this grand festive occasion. The provisions were ample, and much to spare, and so ended this notable gathering in honor of our patriotic service and happy return to our homes, which will ever be cherished by those returned veterans, and we separated forever. The larger share of those men I have never seen since. Quite a number reside in and around Jacksonville. Many, like myself, have found a home in other states; and many have gone to their eternal home. I know of only two who live in Iowa; they are members of my company, and I have had the pleasure of meeting them frequently. I made my home under the paternal roof until November 10, 1865 when I removed to Iowa, which has been my residence ever since, except fifteen months in Kansas. I returned to Iowa in March, 1888.

CHAPTER XIII.

Ever since the close of the war I had a great desire to view again the ground of those mighty operations that resulted in such success to the Union arms and contributed to the perpetuity of our country and its institutions, but my time was so taken up with my ministerial labors and the necessary means to defray expenses was not in hand, so that for thirty years after the war closed I was not able to gratify my desire. The Methodists arranged to hold an International Epworth League Convention at Chattanooga the closing days of June, 1895. The railroads gave reduced rates, so I concluded to go. Rev. F. C. Demorest, of Delta, the secretary of Iowa State Epworth League, and I became traveling companions, and in due time we arrived safely at Chattanooga. There had been great changes wrought since 1863 and 1864, when I was there last. The city then had not more than fifteen hundred inhabitants, it now numbered perhaps forty thousand, and its suburbs took in very largely the positions of the contending armies that fought each other at Lookout Mountain and Missionary Ridge. It was very difficult to find any marks that indicated military occupation or hostile demonstrations. Old Fort Wood that was a ponderous earthwork and mounted thirty-two pounder guns, was quite distinguishable, but the frowning artillery was not there, the rains had washed down the embankments so it did not seem like the formidable structure I had noted thirty-two years before. In Lookout Valley I struggled through brush and briars and found our rifle pits, but very much defaced by the action of the elements and grown up with blackberry briars that were loaded with ripe, luscious fruit I would have been glad to have seen in wartime. I recognized the frowning point of Lookout Mountain, but it was not inclined to belch forth its thunder and death-dealing missiles as of yore. It could now be viewed with complacency and delight, and without fear of loss of limb or life. I recognized also a railway cut across the front of an abrupt foothill, a spur of Lookout where I had stood picket guard and watched the "Johnnies" many times, but, of course, it was all quiet now. But the memory of the past was vivid in presenting the terrible scenes that I had witnessed so long before. The city of Chattanooga presented the usual features of an American city in its buildings and business prospects, not unlike any city of like proportions in the North. But the rural districts and inhabitants seemed scarcely to have undergone any change. The same old houses, many of them very dilapidated, still remained with some few exceptions, and frequently the same people or their children occupied them I had no difficulty in finding the few families I had known when I was there in wartime. The veritable negro with the mule and chain harness, pulled the cart to market as in bygone days. The men wore old style boots with pants thrust inside and the same broad brim wool hat greeted one on every plantation. A lady boarded the train at Chattanooga to go to Shell Mound. She had a little girl, perhaps five years old, with her. Both were neatly and fashionably dressed as any Northern people. When their station was called a large, well-proportioned man, in his shirt sleeves and broad brim hat and big boots and carrying a big ox-gad, was waiting for them at the depot, and a little distance off a sleek, fat yoke of oxen hitched to a large farm wagon with a spring seat on it, was the conveyance that appeared to be in waiting for the lady and little girl. That the tall man with the ox-gad was the lady's husband, I have no doubt, by their greetings, for he caught up the child and bestowed upon her a shower of kisses. I watched them go to the wagon, and after safely seating them he untied his oxen and drove away, to the evident amusement of the passengers, who were mainly from the North, and where transportation by oxen has been out of date for nearly half a century. It had been announced at the first session of the League that a sunrise prayer-meeting (on Lookout) would be part of the program every morning during the convention. So I went up and found about fifteen hundred persons assembled for that purpose. It was very salubrious up there, and the surroundings were quite different to what they were in November, 1863. The services were held near the spot where the Confederate battery was then in position, that threw shot and shell into our camp and Moccasin Point and killed and wounded quite a number of Union soldiers. Now all hostile and murderous features had disappeared, and instead of belching cannon and shrieking shell, we heard the song of praise and fervent prayer addressed to Almighty God for his blessings and the promotion of the Redeemer's kingdom in the hearts of all the brotherhood of man. The contrast was truly striking, and the great change was impressive, indeed. I looked down into the valley and remembered the midnight battle at Wauhatchie, the awful clash of arms and the several hundred men that were killed and wounded; the piteous shrieks of the latter, I could almost fancy still ringing in my ears, and the terrible flashes of cannon and musket-firing breaking forth from all those hills and mountain side. Then after the fearful onset of Longstreet's veterans had been checked and the intrepid Geary hurled his division in unbroken mass against the assailants, they beat a precipitate retreat and all again was quiet. It was a very chilly night and we were hurried out without overcoats and blankets, and when the enemy retired for better security we remained resting on our arms till morning. I do not remember passing a more uncomfortable night in all my army experience than this, and it was some time before we recovered from the fatigue and exposure of that occasion.

Again, as I ate my lunch of sandwiches and bananas and quenched my thirst with refreshing lemonade, I called to mind the six weary days we had subsisted on a scant supply of parched corn, and one Sunday night had scratched the ground for a remnant of scattered corn, where mules had been fed three weeks before, so pressing was the need of that occasion; now how changed. Peace and plenty—even to luxury—on every hand, and instead of thousands of half-starved men, rushing to the fearful onset of murderous battle, thousands of devoted Christians, in religious devotion, were encouraging each other to earnest works of piety and good will to all men. The same old mountain that had witnessed the fury of mortal combat, now, like a silent monitor, took in the reign of nobler peace and seemed to smile in hushed tranquility upon the scene. The next day I visited the field of General Thomas' operations on Missionary Ridge. As near as I could judge, the National Cemetery is located where we first struck the Rebel lines, and from this point we witnessed Hooker's triumph on Lookout Mountain, and just beyond we saw where Wood and Sheridan formed their divisions to assault the enemy's position, and successfully penetrated their works and brought the three days battle to a triumphant close. The old timber growth has disappeared and an entirely new growth has displaced it, much less in density, and I think mainly pine; whereas, at the time of the battle the usual variety of forest trees prevailed. But few traces of the rifle pits and fortifications remain, the electric cars that conserve a more civilized purpose, having wisely been substituted. On the top of the ridge a large iron tower seventy feet high, with winding steps for ascending, stands on the site of Bragg's headquarters. While a substantial, macadamized road is constructed, running continuously with the ridge, marked here and there with cast iron placards to indicate the positions of the various commands that took a part in that momentous struggle. It also retains its war-time significance by many pieces of cannon remaining in position, as if they had been abandoned by the men who so heroically served them during the sanguinary conflict.

On the battleground of Chickamauga many beautiful monuments have been erected by the States having troops there, Ohio, Illinois and Indiana being the main contributors so far in this noble work of commemoration. They are chiefly red and gray granite, with some bronze and marble, all finely executed, and representing in many cases life size statues of soldiers in actual combat. This field is also interspersed with sections of artillery, so placed as to suggest to the tourist their being left where they were actually used. There are three iron towers on Chickamaugua grounds of the same dimensions and pattern as those on Missionary Ridge. I was sensibly impressed by the beautiful arrangement of the National Cemetery at Chattanooga, which contains about twelve thousand of our fallen heroes. It is enclosed with a substantial stone wall, and is accessible from all points of the compass by large iron gates. All the graves are numbered, and as far as possible the soldier's name, company and regiment is given; yet there are many hundreds of those brave men whose last resting-place is indicated by a square marble post, with the mournful word, "Unknown," inscribed as a scanty epitaph to their noble heroism. I here found the graves of sixteen men of my regiment whose last resting-place is contiguous to the imposing monument erected to "Andrews," the famous scout who, with a number of enlisted men, siezed a locomotive at Big Shanty, Georgia, and tried to fire the bridges on the Western and Atlantic Railroad in April, 1862, but who were all captured near Chattanooga, and Andrews and several of his companions were hung. The monument is quite conspicuous and is surmounted by an almost perfect fac simile of the engine used on that occasion. An old soldier has charge of the cemetery and resides on the spot, and it is his duty, and seemed also his pleasure, to impart information to visitors seeking the graves of their friends. A record is kept, alphabetically arranged, of the States and their dead soldiers buried there, and is accessible to all. The grounds are kept in the nicest order, and during the summer months the lawn mower is used frequently, keeping the beautiful sward in the most lovely verdancy.

CHAPTER XIV.

After the adjournment of the convention I took advantage of low rates and went to Atlanta. I witnessed the almost total destruction of that city when Sherman started to the sea, and truly it was a scene of destruction and desolation never before witnessed on this continent and perhaps never will be again. But on its ashes "Phoenix-like," has risen a city of splendor, that so well nigh baffles description that I was unable to make the faintest recognition of any part. In wartimes it was thought to have about eight thousand inhabitants, now it is estimated at sixty-five thousand, and is very compactly built, with all the modern improvements. Here, as at Chattanooga, the electric cars are a prominent feature, displacing the topographical engineering of the military regime. The place marked as the spot of General McPherson's death, was away beyond the defenses of the city. Now it is reckoned within the corporate limits. The part that the 20th corps invested during the temporary siege in August, 1864, I judged to be the site of the extensive buildings of the exposition of 1895, or not very far from it. The city hall, which was one of the most prominent buildings during Sherman's occupation, has been displaced by the much larger and vastly more imposing State capital. I went through this building and made quite an extensive examination. In the collection of paintings I noticed the portraits of most of the prominent heroes of the revolution, as Washington, Marion and others with General Jackson, and some of his cotemporaries. These were placed conspicuously with Jefferson Davis, Gov. Brown, Howell Cobb, Robert Toombs and other famous confederates. These appearing in such bold relief made conspicuous to me the absence of the portraits of Lincoln, Grant and others that usually adorn the capitol buildings of the Northern States.

During my perambulations in this grand building I had a conversation with a native Georgian, a man perhaps sixty years of age, of light complexion and sandy hair, who, I presume, was very much in love with himself and his native state. He scrutinized me closely, and suggested that I was also a pure Georgian, as physically my characteristics were somewhat similar, and his remarks were personally very flattering to me, and perhaps would have made me blush if such things had been said in the presence of ladies. He seemed somewhat taken aback when I told him I was from the State of Iowa and was one of Sherman's bummers. His extravagant personal compliments abruptly terminated; but when I told him I was a native of England he seemed greatly relieved, and soon indicated all the symptoms of anglophobia, and soon began to trace his own descent to the English Cavaliers who had settled Georgia, and who, in his mind, were the purest type of the human race in existence. I was much amused at the old gentleman's racial pride, and of course impressed him that I had met a very distinguished personage, for I had received quite a boom in the ethnological compliments of this scion of Georgia. The people of the South have always accused Northern people of mercenary propensities, but I found there was no lack of money-getting schemes among them, many of them making quite a profitable business in selling relics of the war, some of them tenacious as any Jew to drive a good bargain. It seemed that about one-tenth of the men and boys that I met had scraps of old guns and swords and bullets reputed to have given death-dealing blows in some of the battles, though some of the bullets were remarkably well preserved from the explosive force of the propelling agent. I struck an ingenious fellow that tried to drive a good trade with me by representing that he, too, was a tourist, and gave me a detailed account of a veritable relic, found on Missionary Ridge, where Phil Sheridan's horse leaped the parapet of the rebel works during the battle. He said he wanted a genuine relic, picked up by his own hands on that historic field, but had sought several days and nothing could be found, and in despair he sat at the root of a tree at the point mentioned, and, carelessly digging the ground with a sharpened stick, he struck something that sounded like metal. He then began to dig in earnest, and soon unearthed an old canteen that evidently had been left by some of our men engaged in that battle. He was so elated by his find he said he would not take the world for it, and then he produced the canteen for my inspection. I replied that perhaps it was left by some poor fellow who had lost his life there, and congratulated him on being so fortunate, but my curiosity was not sufficiently aroused to price the relic, at which he seemed disappointed, and soon I began to ply him with questions on other matters. He adroitly turned the subject back to his relic and said really he had picked up so many things that his trunk and grip were full, that he did not know how he was going to "navigate" with the load he had, and he would part with that canteen for a reasonable consideration. I told him I was not such a lover of relics as some people, and he seemed to rate his goods so high that I could not think of ever owning that canteen, no matter how highly I regarded it as a souvenir of Sheridan and the war, for my grasp on real estate was quite limited. This seemed to puzzle him and he asked what I meant. Why, I said, you spoke so earnestly about how you valued it, I dared not think of buying or setting a price on it, for you said you would not take the world for it, and that throws me out of the market, for while I believe in a plurality of worlds, I have not many in my possession yet. He said he was much given to figurative expressions, and of course did not exactly mean that. I then told him my object was not to load myself down with old plunder of any kind, and what he estimated so highly was not worth anything to me, and thoroughly disgusted with his venality, I left him to try his hyperbole methods on some one else.

I visited Grant Park in the south part of the city, which is a creditable illustration of the refined taste of the people of Atlanta. It is not named for the great Union Commander, by any means, but for its chief projector, and whose large donation made it possible, who was a southern man by nativity and characteristics. They have enclosed one of the outward defenses of war times, the cannon are still mounted but show the effects of time and the action of the elements;

the embankments were washed down a good deal, but it was still distinguishable to persons of military experience. On the whole I was quite favorably impressed with Atlanta, and the enterprise and candor of the inhabitants is commendable indeed. I was not so favorably impressed with their haughty demeanor toward the colored people. Their unfairness and cruelty to them seemed a great drawback, and is no doubt one of the lingering traces of the horrid slave system with which they were cursed so many years, and it will probably be generations before it is entirely obliterated. When I boarded a street car at Decatur, an Atlantic suburb, quite a number of passengers got aboard, some of them being professors attached to the Presbyterian University located there. It was rather a sultry morning, and the people seated themselves near the open sides of the car to get the benefit of the cool breezes as much as possible. The first stop we made, three or four respectable-looking colored ladies got on the outside step, but to my surprise no person moved so they could get by, or sit down near the edge of the car. The women looked wishfully for some one to make a move, but made no remarks; a few seconds passed, the white passengers acted as if they were riveted to the seats, and looked daggers at the poor women, who evidently were afraid to speak, while the driver got out of patience and began to curse them.

They then made a move as if they would step off, when one of the white men nearest to them, in a surly manner, moved into the center of the car and opened the way for them to be seated. The gentleman sitting next to me, although, like myself, was not in position to show any courtesies in the matter, was very indignant, and remarked to me: "See how we Southern people have to suffah by those impudent folks. They always try to make themselves conspicuous and humiliate us. They know a great many people from the North are heah, and they just try as much as possible to belittle us. Oh! we have a trying time! You people will never know how much we have to suffah by them." I was moved to say that in this case that I thought the other parties were the afflicted ones; that I thought the humanities of the case, not to say manners, would suggest that the gentlemen near them should have made room for the women to have boarded the car and become seated, as there was plenty of room beyond them, and not exposed them to possible accident, standing on the step while the car was in motion; or, on the other hand, delaying the car, and causing the driver to swear at the non-offending parties, apparently afraid to give reproof where it properly belonged.

I said I never in my life beheld such a travesty on supposed good breeding. At this the college professor (for such he was) shrugged his shoulders, and a'hemmed, and said, ah, well, if you was heah awhile you would soon see those people are unbearable. No one knows what it is to be troubled with them till they try it. I did not venture any farther remarks, and this very delicate subject was dropped. I then asked him in relation to points of interest of their great and prosperous city, and he became more affable, and in a courteous way gave me the desired information. The ex-confederate soldiers seem to have more genuinely accepted the situation of the results of the war than the non-combatants. I conversed with a number of them and without exception I found them reasonable and patriotic men. The experience gained in the war and contact with the Yankee element has had great tendency to disabuse their minds and dispel prejudice and ignorance fostered by the regime of slavery, and they concede it is much better for the country at large to be under one government and one flag than to have two rival governments to indulge in angry bickerings and perhaps be frequently at war over territorial bounderies and other questions. They concede we have a better form of civilization with permanent peace assured, and better protection of person and property, with fast increasing prosperity, than would be were it otherwise. Many of them also concede the great unwisdom of the South beginning the war in the interest of slavery, and risking everything in the appeal to arms with the loyal North, that was so much richer in men and material resources, so that in a contest simply of "might against might" the North was bound to come out ahead, no matter what principles were involved. They also scouted the idea of superior prowess of the Southern people, so much in vogue at the beginning of hostilities—that one Southern man was equal to five Yankees. They know better now, and concede they found "foemen every way worthy of their steel." In a conversation with a man who was a member of Forrest's command and participated in most of the revolting cruelties of that general's warfare, he said if the issue had been left to the common people there would have been no war, and he laid the blame on a few hot-headed politicians on both sides who, he said, egged on the fight, but were very careful to stay out of it themselves. I had heard such remarks in the North, by men of superficial thought, but, in my mind, it lay deeper than the bickerings of hot-headed politicians, and was an "irrepressible conflict" between freedom and slavery that had to be settled, though I did not say so. He said it became very monotonous killing Yankees, without a prospect of exterminating them or so intimidating them they would cease to invade the South. He said it was like killing flies in dy-time, and for every one killed there came hundreds to the funeral, and, no matter how appalling the slaughter of Yankees, there were thousands more to come and avenge their death, and thus, in due time, annihilate the confederates, a possibility I did not presume to gainsay. Another man, who had fought in nearly every battle in the west, from Fort Donalson to the surrender of Johnston's army, said their leaders ought to have known better than to have undertaken such an enterprise in the impoverished condition the South was in, as compared to the full-handed North. He complained of the inferior character of their munitions, and the lack of means to supply an army in provisions and clothing. Such fools, said he, were Jeff Davis and Company. Why, said he, the inferior arms the men had were not worth a dollar and a half apiece; they scarcely pretended to clothe the men or give them a decent supply of food, and their excuse for money (the confederate scrip) was not hardly worth a dollar per wagonload, and how, in all reason, could they expect to overcome the North, that was teeming full of everything, and which had, besides, almost unlimited credit, at home and abroad, as a recognized government and first-class military power, all of which they lacked. As for the niggers, they were not worth fighting for; they had always been a hindrance and a curse to the country, and they always would be, free or otherwise, till they were landed back in Africa or colonized by themselves somewhere; and, for his part, he'd be glad if he never saw one of them again.

But these suggestions only demonstrate the truism of "experience being a dear schoolmaster" and these men, representing the Southern people, could not have come to those sensible conclusions any other way. So if their eyes are now open to perceive the true situation, and they appreciate the Government and love and respect the country and the flag, so as ever to remain patriotic and good citizens. In the language of General Grant, the "war to save the country was worth all it cost," though that consideration was fearful in loss of life and treasure. The people of the South are truly a hospitable people; their kindness to me was quite appreciable, and usually they seemed inclined to great freedom and sociability and, I believe, gave me a welcome to their homes and hearts in consequence of my being in the Northern army. I stopped at a spring in Lookout

Valley, and, while eating a lunch, I was soon joined by a little company of men and women who resided in the immediate neighborhood. They appeared to have come for water, but ostensibly, I think, it was to see who the stranger was. Two of the men were past middle age, and were ex-confederate soldiers. The others were young men and three young women, grown up there since the war. It seemed an occasion of great interest to them to greet me as one of the Yankee soldiers who had taken an active part in military operations there. My conversation seemed very agreeable to them and I enjoyed very much the recital of incidents connected with the war and their neighborhood affairs for a few years after. They pressed me to stay two or three days and share their hospitality and make a more extended tour, a request I was compelled to decline. I was entertained at the home of Mr. James Hammel, who was a boy fourteen years old at the time I was there in 1863. I had some acquaintance with him then, as I had been detained as a safety guard at his father's house at that time. He and his family were glad to see me. His wife was a native of Georgia, and gave me a sketch of her life. She said her father, before the war, was in affluent circumstances, had a good estate and owned slaves, and she was raised in easy circumstances up to her twenty-second year, when the war came. She had not known how to do a thing, only to be waited on by the servants. But the misfortunes of war caused her father to lose everything, and when she married Mr. Hammel he was a laboringman, and she had also to go to work and help make the living. She did not know how to sew or wash, or even sweep the floor, and knew even less about the art of cooking. "But,"said she, I was willing to work, and now I think I am a pretty good housekeeper and cook, too, considering I had to learn everything I know after I was married. Don't you think so, Mr. Potter?" I remarked her comfortable home and her very palatable meals was abundant confirmation of what she said, which seemed to please her very much, for she had a good degree of honest pride in her accomplishments, and not without very good reasons therefore. I was surprised to note that the farmers had not kept pace with the times in availing themselves of the improved implements for agricultural purposes and usually farmed on a very small scale as compared to Iowa and Illinois. Ten acres of corn was a large crop for one man to take care of. They use the single shovel plow with the ever almost omnipresent mule and rope and chain gears (as they call them—they would not know what was intended by the word harness if it was used in their hearing.) I saw men busy taking in the oats harvest, swinging the cradle, a process that many of our Northern young people never saw in their lives. Up in Tennessee, near the Kentucky line, I saw a reaper at work—the old style Champion self-rake—such as the farmers of Iowa abandoned a quarter of a century ago, and in nearly everything I noticed these clever-hearted people adhered to old-time customs and plodded along, apparently as happy as the tireless, go-ahead people of the North. These things indicate that they live too far back in the remote past to enjoy a profitable income from the amount of labor they are compelled to put upon a vastly less productive soil than the fertile prairies of Iowa or Illinois.

The people of the South seem loth to give up those simple and time-honored customs, and do not appreciate any remarks that disparage those antiquated usages that seem so comical to Northern people. At one of the stations where the train was detained a few minutes a man drove up with a team composed of a large, ungainly mule and a very skeleton-looking cow, hitched to a large farm cart, he with his wife and children filling it to the utmost capacity, and altogether presenting a very grotesque appearance, which provoked a great deal of merriment among the passengers, who were mainly tourists from the North. A dignified, clerical-looking gentleman on the other side of the car seemed pained at the jocularity of our party. I spoke to him and inquired if he was from the North, and he gave me a very decided negative, and informed me he was from South Carolina, and had been attending the Epworth League Convention at Chattanooga and was on his homeward journey. As he seemed somewhat piqued at the hilarity of the other passengers, I ventured to remark, apologetically, that there were many features of Southern life so radically different from the North that it seemed to strike them on the ludicrous side of their natures, and it was difficult to abstain from remarks of a mirthful character. He remarked, "I perceive your company is inclined to be very boisterous." I said it was never seen in the North—two different animals, as the cow and mule, yoked together for a team, and hence the pleasantry of our party. Yet, said he, solemnly, cultivated Christian people should never make sport of the misfortunes of the poor, and he considered it a breach of decorum for professing Christians to indulge in boisterous laughter, simply because a man could not drive two mules, and had to substitute his cow by reason of abject poverty. I saw he was a very serious man, and, in fairness, must acknowledge his strictures were well taken; and yet I could not restrain my risibilities at the sight of such an incongruous means of transportation as our eyes were now beholding.

The few days I spent on these historic grounds were replete with pleasure to me, and I could have agreeably remained and enjoyed the varied scenes of that picturesque and salubrious clime for many days, but time forbade, and with some lingering regrets that I had not arranged for a more prolonged stay, I boarded the cars and was soon speeding homeward.

Memorial Sermon.

Preached at Montezuma, Iowa, May 25, 1895.

TEXT: "Other men labored, and ye are entered into their labors."—John 4:38.

In the providence of God some men sustain the relation of benefactors to the human race in general. In the prosecution of their labors they frequently experience privation and suffering that is incidentally connected with great personal sacrifice, for which they receive no adequate material compensation, and have no reward, save the consciousness of having rendered their fellow-beings a lasting benefit, while society has greatly benefited by the success achieved through their devotion and unrequited toil. Columbus gave to the world the greatest discovery it has ever known. It was brought about by patient study and intense application to purpose, amid great difficulty and opposition, under which the indomitable nature of the great navigator never shrank, but persevered till glorious success crowned his efforts.

It is not strange that the dream of Empire and vast emoluments should have a place in the thought of a man who could in that period project such a colossal enterprise, and we may pardon Columbus for the seeming avarice in indicating terms to his Royal Patrons that were only commensurate with the vastness of the discovery, his remarkable penetration and genius, placed in the line of almost assured realization. His obscure origin and slender means should heighten general admiration and secure the unqualified approbation of all mankind.

But in the realization of proper reward he was doomed to disappointment and cruel treatment; envious men breathed reproach and calumny against him, and he was unjustly imprisoned and loaded with chains, and, only fourteen years after his great discovery, having passed through great sufferings, and in the midst of wretched poverty, he died, "unhonored and unsung."

In the settlement of our western frontier no man rendered as great service as Daniel Boone. With his trusty rifle, he plunged into the forest wilds of Kentucky, and led the van guard of civilization into that unbroken wilderness, his experience as a hunter and Indian fighter qualifying him for the dangerous service he rendered. His personal sacrifices were very great, and in these sanguinary struggles with the "Red men of the Forest" he sustained many losses and hair-breadth escapes, the blood of his own family commingling with the soil of that disputed territory. By these he rendered an invaluable service, and was entitled to a generous share of the domain which, largely through his prowess, had been won from the savage control of the Indians. But the legal powers of Kentucky, through some slight technicality of law, dispossessed him of all his claims, and in his advanced years he was compelled to leave his Kentucky home and plunge into the "wilds" of Missouri for a lodging place, disgusted at the ingratitude and injustice of his fellow men.

Another class of men that render society great and lasting benefit are the real inventors, whose genius, materialized, has done so much to utilize the elements of nature and conduce to the comfort and happiness of men. Yet, almost without exception, they failed to realize equitable compensation for their indefatigable labor in bringing about their invaluable discoveries. Charles Goodyear conceived the project of utilizing caoutchouc, or India rubber. Amid poverty, and despising the jeers of his neighbors, who thought him a crank, he battled through penury and inappreciation so appalling as to cause one to shudder at the thought of them; yet he persevered through all these disparagements, and finally he was rewarded with complete success. But the patient inventor was lacking in financial ability to secure the pecuniary value of his invention. Other designing men seized upon it and made independent fortunes. It added a new and valuable industry to the world's commodities, and thousands of persons are now dependent upon it for a means of livelihood, and general society has enjoyed great immunity of relief from its multifarious application to the purposes of life, while Goodyear was relegated to comparative poverty.

The achievement of American independence is considered a gracious boon, not only to America, but to mankind in general, in its results and far-reaching possibilities. The patriotic devotion and sacrifices of the Revolutionary Fathers is almost without a parallel in the history of nations, when we consider carefully the nature of the enterprise, in presuming to cope with Great Britain, the foremost military power of the time, involving a seven years' war, impoverishing and devastating in character. The hardships and sufferings of that period are truly heartrending to contemplate and are an indication of the courageous spirit of the fathers, who pledged their fortunes, their lives and their sacred honor for so worthy a cause. It is one of the most difficult things to arrange the logistics for an army engaged in active hostilities, since steam and electricity have been brought to conserve in rapid transit of intelligence and supplies; but how much greater in that earlier period of our country's history must have been the difficulty of marshaling an army and supplying it adequately for efficient service. So, Washington's Army was often reduced to the greatest extremities, and was half-starved and poorly clad, and unpaid a great deal of the time during the struggle for independence. Yet this did not deter them from persevering in their noble purpose; neither did they consider how small must be their share of the inestimable benefits of the revolution. So we conclude that our fathers, who through seven years of sanguinary war, secured freedom and independence for this continent, yet did not reap to themselves adequate compensation for their patriotic devotion to their country's welfare.

Only fifty years after Great Britain conceded the independence of the Colonies, Daniel Webster, at the unveiling of Bunker Hill Monument, made an address to the survivors of the revolution when scarcely a corporal's guard of them remained to represent the heroes who had followed Washington through his remarkable career.

At this time the population of the United States was about 15,000,000 as against 3,000,000 that comprised the population of the country during the revolution. If we make a necrological deduction, as we may fairly, of one-half, it would give us 13,500,000 inhabitants that were enjoying the benefits of American freedom, who had not borne the slightest burden of military duty to secure the governmental blessing they enjoyed. We come now to consider the great deliverance of our country from the Slaveholders' Rebellion of 1861, an event fraught with such tremendous results that the revolution itself is hardly worthy of a just comparison, though it ushered in the birth of a great Nation. It is no sacrilege if I quote from the old hymn, "'Twas great to speak a world from naught,'twas greater to redeem." So, while we take pleasure in calling Washington the Father of his Country, we are also pleased to term Lincoln the Savior of the Nation, and its salvation from its determined domestic foes is even more important than the success of the revolution. The mighty and valorous deeds of the men who saved the Nation from its internecine foes, involved the severest ordeal of labor, exposure and danger, and almost unheard of privation, testing alike the mental and physical faculties to the utmost, that has no parallel in the affairs of ordinary civil pursuits. The formidable proportions of the secession movement inaugurated by Jefferson Davis and his coadjutors—eleven

States seceded, and what little Union sentiment remained was so crushed and feeble as to make the South practically a unit in the scheme of rearing a slave oligarchy on the ruins of the Union, and pledging their lives, their fortunes and their sacred honor to this purpose, made the most formidable foe the government of the United States has ever encountered, and called forth the most stupendous military preparations ever beheld on the Western Hemisphere. Then the vast extent of territory of those States—an empire in area—with the natural obstructions of mountain ranges and deep and rapid rivers, susceptible of being easily fortified and made well-nigh impregnable to an hostile army, so that in defensive warfare the South had very superior advantages over the North, of not less than two to one. In the four years' war it is estimated that two thousand battles and skirmishes were fought by the respective belligerents; of these perhaps twenty would compare favorably with the battle of Waterloo in point of numbers engaged and sanguinary results. This battle decided the fate of the great Napoleon Bonaparte, whose military successes had been the terror of all Europe for years. And by making this contrast we are able to conceive of the very enduring qualities of the American soldier, who survived these awful scenes of carnage, and, with calm intrepidity, prepared for another onset. Again, let us consider the long and frequent marches made by the Union troops. You business men and others, whose feats of pedestrianism are measured by a few hundred yards, and for long journeys you employ the "iron horse," and shorter ones the faithful horse, in easy carriages, sets you down at your destination, without fatigue or detriment of any kind, or you use the whirling bicycle to avoid the wear and tear of natural locomotion. Just consider that the marches of the "Boys in Blue" involved distances of hundreds and thousands of miles. It is usually conceded that the 15th Army Corps compassed the greatest distance of any command in the army, and it is a reasonable estimate to place the aggregate at four thousand miles, while the 20th Corps, with which I served, marched more than twenty-five hundred, in all kinds of weather and over all sorts of roads, wading swamps and streams, almost innumerable. The privations connected with this service involve separation from all endearing ties of civilized society, the genial company of relatives and friends, the sacred and hallowed influences of home and religious associations. The endearing love of mother, wife, sister, sweetheart, and other friends is subordinated to the "love of country," which is supposed to conquer. Not that the soldier forsakes these loves, but he is deprived of their society, their tender helpfulness and restraining influence, to militate the coarser tendencies of camp life and isolation from civilizing agencies. The allowance of food is of the plainest sort, and is usually of two or three staple articles, as coffee, bread, meat, and beans for breakfast, beans for dinner, beans for supper, beans, beans, beans, "adinfinitum," and sometimes even some of these were lacking. Rosecran's army, at Chattanooga, was compelled to subsist for a number of days on a scant supply of parched corn, and the awful extremities to which our prisoners were reduced at Andersonville and other places is too well known to be repeated here.

The exposure to filth and disease, for the most part, is beyond expression. I will just add the expression of a returned soldier: "I would not have again the experience with vermin for the largest pension paid for disability." While it is well known that thousands of men, exposed to contagious diseases, either lost their lives or returned physical wrecks, to suffer untold agonies the residue of their days. The carnage of battle is also awful to contemplate. We may mention the large number of men placed "hors de combat" in a few notable battles. The number of killed and wounded at Shiloh was 15,000; Murphysboro, 12,000; Chickamauga, 19,000; Fredericksburg, 15,000; Gettysburg, 23,000, and the Wilderness, 18,000; and, in the aggregate of all battles during the war, more that 300,000, and 200,000 may be estimated as dying of wounds and disease contracted in the service, within a very few years after the close of the war, making a grand total of a half million of men who lost their lives by the civil war.

Let us now consider the benefits accruing to the valorous men who were subjected to these terrific ordeals for the salvation of our country. The half million of patriots who yielded their lives upon the field of battle, or in the hospital, or shortly after returning to their homes—they have retired beyond the reach of human reward or material emoluments. Neither governments nor individuals can reward the dead. They gave their lives; they received absolutely nothing in return. The gratitude that finds its expression in expensive monuments erected to their honor, and fragrant flowers strewed upon their graves on Memorial Day, is nothing to them (while it is proper and sentimental for the living beneficiaries to show these tokens of patriotic regard). They are so circumstanced with the environments of an eternal world; where gold is dross and earth's best gifts are so beggarly as to be without significance and without value. The number of physically disabled by wounds or disease is also great. Yet is permanent loss of health mitigated or redressed by pecuniary compensation? Is partial or entire blindness susceptible of being actually palliated by dollars and cents? Would any person in their senses yield the organs of seeing or hearing for any consideration? Would a man part with a leg or an arm for any amount of gold, or its equivalent? Satan is represented as saying, in the book of Job: "Skin for skin; yea, all that a man hath will he give for his life." And if it did come from an unworthy source, it is a truism. The physical faculties as well as the mental are the unpurchasable requisites of every human being, and all of these were laid upon the altar of our country's service by every faithful soldier who was killed or maimed or emaciated by disease, either dying or returning home to eke out the residue of his days in untold suffering, or, having escaped from all the perils of war, served honorably in every line of duty he was called to perform. Hence, these patriotic men placed at the disposal of the government their personal requisites, which, if deprived of them in the casualities of war, could not be replaced by governmental prerogative. So that the logical and moral sequence is clearly to make the government a lasting debtor to the noble veterans who saved it from the assaults of the Confederate armies. The men who were fortunate enough to escape the injuries and fatalities of war, when the sword was sheathed and the roaring cannon was hushed by the surrender at Appomattox, soon all returned to the pursuits of civil life, and asked no boon aside from the privileges of a common citizen, in which soldier and civilian should share alike, and, with scarcely an exception worth naming, these veterans of the civil war have assumed cheerfully the burdens of citizenship and conducted themselves honorably and creditably as members of our great commonwealth. That these have equitable claims upon the government for their eminent services all fair-minded and patriotic men will concede; but can they be suitably rewarded? The life of a nation that we may hope shall endure a thousand years, secured by the excessive toil and endurance through indescribable privation and untold suffering. What is the little pension money, doled out so grudgingly, at the rate of two to seventy dollars per month, accordingly as the pensionable character of the applicant may be fixed, by a board of fallable surgeons, compared to what the government or the great body politic has received. The courage, sacrifices and services that saved our nation and perpetuated its liberties and institutions cannot be estimated by the ratio of filthy lucre. Great as has been our country's prosperity and increase in all material resources, it will always be too poor to pay for its life. It can, in a feeble measure, contribute a part of its substance to ease the veterans' declining years as they travel along life's rugged journey. It can aid in keeping the "wolf from the door," and feed and clothe the indigent survivors of the war; but it cannot restore sight to the blind, hearing to the deaf, nor health to the permanently impaired soldier. It cannot raise the dead; it cannot give back to weeping mothers their darling sons; it cannot return to the mourning widow her husband and protector, who went down "the valley of the shadow of death" in its behalf. Who has, in the largest degree, profited by the preservation of the Union and institution of popular government that obtains in the United States by reason of the success of the Federal armies? The millions of our population that now in peace and prosperity enjoy all the rights and privileges of a great and free government. In 1860 the population of our country was 30,000,000, the Northern States having about 20,000,000 of these, from whom, in the main, the Union armies were recruited. It is safe to estimate that one half of the 20,000,000 have crossed the "dark and mysterious river," leaving 10,000,000. If we add to these one-half of the population of the South, or 5,000,000, allowing the same percentage of death rate, we have, in the aggregate, 15,000,000 survivors of the census of 1860. Now, as the increase of population reaches the enormous figures of 70,000,000, we have 55,-000,000 of people enjoying "life, liberty and the pursuit of happiness" under our constitution and our flag that have come upon the stage of action and emigrated from foreign lands since the return of peace in 1865. Truly the government is practicallly in the hands of this mighty population so recently come into the rights of citizenship in our favored country. By the ballot box these can decree who shall minister this government, what shall be its legislation and reforms, and in what manner shall the claims of the war-worn and aged veterans be redressed. That as a great and appreciative people value the blood-bought privileges they enjoy through the patriotic services of the dead and the fast retiring column of the surviving veterans, may we not hope that those enjoying the noblest grade of citizenship this side of heaven, will, in equity, in unfeigned patriotism, do right, be broad, be liberal, and, with appreciative magnanimity, care for those who have borne the burden of unspeakable sanguinary conflict for the present generation and for all time and posterity. But let me exhort my comrades in arms, who, on the threshold of time and seeing the dawn of an eternal day beaming upon us, let us, without ostentation, submit to all the providences in store for us, and, as we proved the character of our manhood as the saviors of a nation, let us, as worthy citizens, peaceably do the same. And, while our declining years accumulate in burdens and sufferings as we await the call of the final "muster out," let us not expect too much of the government. Be it ever so rich and great, yet, like all human institutions, its resources are limited and exhaustible. There is no adequate compensation this side of the grave for the patriotic sacrifices it required to save and perpetuate a nation's life. For the full bounty of reward we must draw upon the infinite resources of heaven itself. If we make a confident friend of the Eternal Father, who seest not as men see, "whose thoughts are higher than our thoughts," "whose ways are higher than our ways," "who is not unrighteous to forget your labor of love," "in whose presence is fulness of joy," "at whose right hand there are pleasures forever more," He will reward liberally! He will reward as the King of Kings and Lord of Lords! "He spared not his own son; shall he not, with him, freely give us all things?" If we are truly contrite in heart, and, by sincere faith, put our hand into the hand of our Saviour, who is also the King of Heaven, he will gently lead us through this rugged "vale of tears, and in the great final mustering day, with all the angelic host, "Shout us welcome to the skies."

www.ingramcontent.com/pod-product-compliance
Lightning Source LLC
Chambersburg PA
CBHW020840160426
43192CB00007B/725